Other Books by the Author

In the Age of Youth

Living on Dreams

The Story of Teeny Tiny Tammy

A Gringo's Tour of Mazatlán

Marinating in Dream Sauce

Sleeping Under the Bandstand

Photo Books by the Author

The Alchemist's Guide;
to Salted Paper Printing

The Alchemist's Guide;
to The Kallitype Print

The Alchemist's Guide;
Printing in Palladium

The Alchemist's Guide;
to Printing with Gum

Alchemist's Guide:

To Black & White Photo Chemistry

Principles and Procedures
for Negative & Print Development

Grant M. Handgis

Brother Coyote Publications

For

Those photographers who treasure the knowledge of their craft

2nd Edition

https://www.gmichaelhandgisphotography.com;
Email: gmhandgis@gmail.com

Grant M. Handgis,
Alchemist's Guide | Photographic Book

Brother Coyote Publications

B.C.P

ISBN - 13: 978-0692453476
ISBN -10: 0692453474

Author's Note

I have been writing this book, in my head, for almost thirty years. It is the accumulation of my experiences as a black and white photographer working with black and white film, and printing papers. When I began developing black and white film, the digital process had yet to be conceived.

I had been photographing since the sixties, using a small plastic camera equivalent to the Kodak Brownie. I used that camera to shoot my first series of images, of my little sister in a cowgirl outfit harnessing our Beagle up to a wagon using a jump rope, then climbing onto the wagon for the final image of her as buckboard queen. That, for me, began the process of pre-visualization.

The book I had in mind had to do with cutting through the extraneous portions of the photographic process. What I envisioned was a simple manual that explained black and white photography simply as a process. That process is not a rigid one. The very essence of black and white photography is that it is malleable, and is capable of being altered and defined by the photographer.

What I have set out to accomplish with this book is to offer the photographer working with black and white film a path to follow to achieve a fine print. As explained through the book, this process can be altered at different stages to achieve desired results specific to the photographer's pre-visualized concept of the image, via the final print. All this can be achieved following the basic procedures that follow.

In black and white photography, there is no one *correct* way of processing and printing. There should only be *your* way, *your* vision that uses the chemistry process to achieve it. The only boundaries being the unknown.

Table of Contents

Author's Note i
Table of Contents ii, iii
Acknowledgment iv
Forward v
Opening ~ To Photographers 1
Part I ~ The Negative 11
Diagram 1 ~ Film Emulsion Graphic 12
Diagram 2 ~ Time/Density Relationship Graphic 13
Resolution Factors 15
Acutance Factors 16
Contrast Index Chart 18
Diagram 3 ~ D LogE Curve ~ W/Densities 22
Part 2 ~ Controls of The Negative 27
Texture Tests 29
Metering for Black and White 30
Diagram 4 ~ D LogE Curve ~ Textural Zones 33
Part 3 ~ Black and White Photo Chemistry 39
Section 1 ~ Chemical Constituents 40
Reducers ~ 43
Preservatives ~ 47
Accelerators ~ 49
Restrainers ~ 50
Section 2 ~ Formulas 53
Formula: Beutler 105 ~ 53
Diagram 3 ~ 3 Beutler CI Curves 56
As a function of Dilution Rates 56
Expansions ~ Compactions 57

Formula: D-23 59
Formula: Windish Pyro 62
Formulas: Pyrocatechin Formulas 64-67
Formula: D-76 68
Section 3 ~ Stop Baths & Fixers 71
Stop Baths 72
Formula: Stop Baths ~ Hardening Formulas 73
Fixing Baths 74
Formulas: Non-Hardening Fixing Baths 75
Formulas: Hardening Fixing Baths 77-78
Charts: Clearing Times for Fixing Baths 80
Chart: Exhaustion Rates for Fixing Baths 80
Hypo Remover 81-82
Part 4 ~ The Print 89
Formulas: Cool Tone Developers 89
Formulas: Warm Toned Developers 90-91
Formula: Amidol 92
Formulas: Pyrocatechin Developers 93-94
Formula: Freemesser 2-Bath Developer 95
Part 5 ~ Equivalents ~ Weights & Measures 100-107
Negatives Formulas 108-112
Stop Baths 113
Fixing Baths 114-116
Clearing Times Fixing Baths 116-117
Print Formulas 118-124
Dilution to Dilution Chart 126
Diagram: Cut Film Holders for Texture Tests 127
Part 6 ~ Bibliographic References 131

Acknowledgment

The cover of this book was designed by the author. The cover photo was taken by the author while living in Eugene, OR, thirty years ago. This image was one of many, capturing elements of the Oregon forests and rivers of that time.

The photograph on the cover is unique, and remains in the author′s collection. The graphs and charts in this book were created by the author. Any replication of a graph from a publication was done with properly assigned credits. The graphs are for demonstrative purposes and are not to scientific scale.

Forward

Black and white photography can be an art form. One that endures after more than a century of acceptance by galleries and museums, and collectors. The practical application of photography has evolved over that same century, with ever advancing technological breakthroughs in camera equipment, as well as with film and paper emulsions. What has not changed are the practices and procedures that produce the images of the finished print.

Although film and paper emulsions have changed over the years, the interaction between the silver halide in the emulsions and the chemistry that reduces them, remains the same. This book is meant as a reference manual, a guide that allows the photographer to see the process as a whole, even before snapping the photograph. Every choice made, from clicking the shutter to hanging up the finished print potentially alters that final image.

This book is for those photographers who wish to control the process themselves, by developing their own negatives. It has been laid out in a sequential order to the fuller process, which I believe begins before snapping the photograph. I am a believer in the holistic approach of understanding all the elements of shaping the photographic image, to arrive at a personalized expression of the image.

The craft of black and white photography, like any art form, allows for a wide range of potential expressions, if the photographer understands the tools of the craft. That is the purpose of this book. The tools at hand are not difficult to use or understand, even for one new to the developing process. I spent years learning the finer points of developing negatives and prints, through understanding the chemistry that made that happen. It is a worthwhile endeavor.

The connection between the printer and the final print, is more than a photographic process. For success, the printer is the process.

The Author

Alchemist's Guide;

To Black & White Photo Chemistry

This book is dedicated to those photographers who have never given up their aspirations for achieving their photographic artistry, utilizing traditional photographic processes and respective processing practices. Black and white photography remains an art form that is practiced throughout the country, the world at large. With the advent of digital photography, photography has changed, in the social sphere, as it has so many times before. Each new advent of technology alters the current application(s) of photography in different ways.

Having spent ten years as a commercial photographer using digital photography has shown itself to be very handy, for commercial photographers as well as the average person, with automatic cameras for $100, that can zoom out effectively as a 500mm lens or more, with images recorded at 20mgp, representing a digital image at over 300 dpi for print quality images. However, speaking as one who has attempted to continue thirty years of black and white photography, as art, I found I was losing interest in this form of photography.

I just happen to be one of those photographers who is very bad at digital applications to visual images, photographic or otherwise. I don't do stick people well enough for them to pass as stick people. I spent my photographic life behind the lens. In the early years, while living in Eugene, Oregon, I carried a Burke & James 5x7 flatbed camera, replete with all the accouterments necessary for a rewarding day of photographing in the world.

Twenty years later I was carrying a Cannon E series DSLR, shooting events for a living. For commercial uses, I can't see going back to film. When you're shooting more than 600 high school or college graduates rushing across stage to grab their diploma and run off to party, does not make a good case for reloading a camera every 36 clicks of the shutter.

Those years were hard-sweat workdays compared to continuously clicking the shutter of a digital camera, into an 8-gig CF card, hundreds of times, without moving, then downloading it all into a computer in seconds. With digital, the shooter also knows immediately if the image was indeed captured as expected.

However, for me, when it comes to Art, that is an entirely different objective, and outcome. A hand printed Gel Silver print is likely going to remain a more desirable print for collectors than a Giclee′ print, on its own. Only name recognition will alter that. A Giclee′ print of Edward Weston′s "Pepper" print is going to sell for more than most Gel Silver prints without the name draw, but not if the same name draw was to put up the two types of their prints side by side.

For me, black and white photography is "Real" photography. A refrain I used during the days of carrying the field camera. Hence, this book. It is entertaining when I make that comment in larger photographic circles these days with both digital, and color shooters. This is not a slight on color photography, as there are many very beautiful examples of fine color work.

For the most part, a color photograph is a representation of the world it has captured. The world as we see it through our own eyes. Black and white photography shifts the image in a transformational way, a more dramatic replication of things that alters the viewer's perception of the image, different from the world as normally perceived.

It might be said that there are differences between black & white, and color shooters. This isn′t a good or bad, right or wrong thing, but a natural, artistic perceptual difference. Every photographer has their own artistic eye and photographic instinct to guide them, and direct their endeavors. It is that which keeps the range of art work healthy.

A bit of history. When my good photographer friend, Larry Gellert, and I formed a photography gallery, The Gelhan Gallery, in the spring of 1984, we sent out a call to all photographers for a meeting, with our intent of finding potential candidates to recruit for the gallery. Our mistake. A stupid one that taught us a great deal about recruiting, photographers, and human nature.

What we were interested in achieving, and were recruiting for, were black and white photographers. Our business plan was to focus on collectable black and white photographs, specializing in black and white photography and print making. Simple goal, expressed poorly. Neither of us had any interest in artistic color photographs, for more than one reason.

The primary reason was simply that both of us were dedicated followers of the craft of black and white photography, driven to learning every phase of processing necessary to achieve a fine art print. We were inspired and motivated by earlier photographic pioneers before us. Larry was inspired by Edward Weston's work and my inspiration derived from Alfred Stieglitz and his "Secessionist's" movement.

When we tried to get that basic tenet across to the now rowdy crowd at the photographer's meeting, it didn't go over well, at all. We were accused of being elitist, narrow minded, counterproductive, and a couple of other invectives better left unmentioned. We did find twelve photographers who photographed exclusively in black and white, had been doing so on average for ten years, and had good bodies of work with finished portfolios of mounted archival prints. Our kind of photographers.

Back then, digital wasn't a concept yet known, Film was the only game in town and it was but a decision as to what type of film one wanted to use. A primary objection to color photographs back then was simply longevity. C-prints had a color fidelity of under ten years, on a wall, possibly a bit more in an album. At best.

The only color fidelity option at the time was the Cibachrome process, which is "a dye destruction positive-to-positive photographic process used for the reproduction of film transparencies on photographic paper. The prints are made on a dimensionally stable polyester base as opposed to traditional paper base." (Google) Hence, image stability and archival longevity of over a hundred years. Some say twice that.

There were plenty of galleries that hung Cibachrome prints on their walls back then. There were no galleries that dedicated their walls strictly to black and white photographs, including historical hand coated prints, in short limited editions. That was a second tenet of our gallery. No print would ever be sold in open edition. That, for us, does not represent a collectable print. Little more than a hand printed poster. Speaking for myself, any print sold as "Art" should have an edition count noted on the print, and a printed certificate of authenticity to back it up. All prints sold through our gallery were in certified editions not exceeding (25).

That at first had not been a prerequisite for being represented by the gallery, nor hang there. That practice simply caught on among the photographers and everyone came on board that practice. One of the photographers that joined later, making it the thirteenth member, was Claire Trotter, a photographer whose photographs hung in New York and

Chicago museums, as well as several large, private and corporate collections. Having her ask me if she could join the gallery was one of the two highlights of my years owning that gallery. I will mention the second one, later.

During one of the visits with her at her house in Eugene, I asked her if she had ever sold more than twenty-five copies of any one image in her sixty years as a photographer. She pondered a moment then said, "no." I then asked her if she might be willing to address that directly and make plain the edition limit, and print number, on each print, and allow me to issue a certificate of authenticity for each print sold through the gallery. She liked the idea, and that practice was implemented and applied thereafter.

Due to a turn of events in life, my gallery partner found the need to take his leave from the gallery to focus on his family. That left me with a new and untested gallery to keep afloat, and functioning. Confessions as they are, that scared me silly. I had only been a working photographer for a scant few years and still a bit new with black and white photo chemistry. Not to fear, hold onto the reins with both hands and let the horses run until they're tired. All would work out. When asked how that works, I can only repeat that great line... "It's a mystery."

The Gelhan Gallery became the g. Michael Handgis Gallery, and continued the day to day operations with the owner on a very steep learning curve, running as fast as was possible. Being run on a shoestring budget using chewing gum and duct tape to hold things together, the gallery lasted a bit longer than two years, until the fire.

What I learned in those precious years was simply that Alfred Stieglitz's vision of photography as art, holds true even in today's world of super digital technology. In today's world of magical devices one can easily alter color to black and white (panchromatic) with a tap on a menu of the camera, or using photo editing software. It is not that one has all those options at their disposal, but if one chooses to use that model of photography in general. There is no *correct* method. Just one's preferred method.

There are digital photographers and there are traditional method photographers. Film shooters, and from what I glean from the current temperature is that they are quite proud of it too. I have utilized digital photography commercially for ten years before I finally retired as a commercial photographer in 2010. Having the luxury of time, after that, for pondering questions of the heart, and photography, I have come to realize some important aspects about photography in general, and traditional photography in particular.

When I refer to as *traditional* photography, I refer to black and white photography using film, chemical processing, followed by either contact printing or enlargement, onto Silver Gelatin papers. That is what this book is about, black & white film and the photo chemistry that controls it. That technical methodology goes back uninterrupted for over a century. Tradition. As I mentioned, my photographic mentor during my early years of photography was Alfred Stieglitz. I believed in his methodology for keeping photography into two camps. The *professional-commercial* and *amateur artist*. I have no doubt my distinction might draw some criticism, but that is what I came away from concerning his historical work and documentation.

Alfred believed that if one approached the craft of photography as an artist, following the dictates and demands of museum quality artwork, then it could be said that photography *can* be art. No guarantees though. That's the short version of the argument, and I have no doubt it continues in more than one photo salon to this day.

I have seen very beautiful, large, digitally printed images. I've done so myself many times, mostly using Epson printers and Red River Fine Art papers. The prints can be very beautiful. In itself, that's a good thing. I ask, have you ever put a Giclee' print next to a Silver Gelatin print, side by side? Or seen a late model fiber-based Gel Silver print next to a 30's era silver-enriched paper, from the days of 'Gas Light' papers, when silver was saturated in the emulsion. The difference between each of the above prints is simply the visual differences, and they stand out.

I had the pleasure of perusing through the gallery in Old Town San Diego, where Alfred Eisenstaedt has his work housed. His prints from the sixties were of course beautiful. But it was his prints pre 50's and late 30's that were stunning. Deep, endless blacks, miles of middle silvery middle tones and crisp whites with full texture. Just made me grin like a fool standing there ogling those beautiful prints, in a price range one might see in the window of a luxury automobile. The print of the New York street scene of a sailor kissing the nurse after WWII is bumping up against $50K now.

The most obvious difference between those prints was the amazing textural quality of the older prints.

I have a close photography friend in New Mexico who continues to actively pursue his photography as Art, building his body of work and producing beautiful prints. He has also seen the double whammy of digital photography explode over the past years. The inexpensive little pocked automatic camera showed up and my work as a Event Photography almost disappeared when I was actively shooting. Who needed a photographer when you just grab this little digital throw away camera and do it myself, or let the party member have at it....

And for me, therein lies the later problem, of selling your digital artwork. Everyone and anyone can do it today. Push a button, on the automatic or cell-phone, plug it in or wi-fi it, plop the image in photo software and auto-fix, then hit the print button on an inexpensive printer and there is your photograph on archival paper. Good for over 100 years. Is that Art? Yep, that's up to you.

My argument for the sanctity of traditional photography has to do with the simple fact not everyone can do it, want to or not. There's the little problem of having access to a darkroom, then actually knowing what you are doing when you get there to arrive at a fine art print. You actually have to know your craft to make it to that fine art print stage.

There will be sections in this book on every aspect of black & white photography, from a section on the Negative, a section on photo chemistry, fixing for the negative and the print, developing times, printing techniques like split bath printing, contrast index and understanding the D LogE curve and how to control it.

I did not go to a Photography School, and certainly do not have an MFA in Photography, thank you. I am self-taught, over the course of thirty years as a professional photographer. Five of those years spent in intense study of black and white photo chemistry, theory and practice, and producing fine art prints. That was also the time I owned the photographic gallery in Eugene, Oregon, representing the thirteen fine art photographers

I was fortunate to have a custom darkroom on the side of my house, behind the studio I made out of a carport enclosure project. The darkroom was an 8ft x 10ft room, with eight-foot stainless steel rinsing sink, chemical mixing table with utility shelf above, and a large print table with a Durst 4x5 projector enlarger. I also had a closet for keeping dry chemicals and other supplies. I was lucky. So very lucky.

Having moved, giving up my darkroom, it was almost twenty years later that I put together a custom darkroom, after retirement, when this book was written. That darkroom is larger, and now configured to make hand coated prints exclusively. I built a custom UV printer that now prints 11x14 palladium and gum over palladium prints. This book will be focused on black & shite negatives to be used for printing on silver gelatin papers.

For those that have such luxuries to work with are the lucky ones. And at this time the few and the special. Blessedly, you are becoming an anachronism, from which beautiful Art continues to be printed and exhibited. This book is for you black and white enthusiasts and active photographers who continue to use black and white films, and traditional darkroom techniques. It is for you that I put this collection of photographic information into one book, my thirty years of study and application.

It is not my intent to disparage digital photography. It is here to stay and has its place in the photographic historical timeline. There are always tradeoffs in technological advancements. One nice tradeoff is there is no need to carry a large field camera in order to arrive at a large negative. Now, it is simple enough to take any sized negative and scan it to garner a very high-resolution replica of the image, scaled to any size desired; within limits. No need to carry a bulky 5x7 flatbed camera to be able to print to 16x20, either through enlargement or contact printing.

In my thinking, even if one photographs in a digital mode, then "develops" by manipulating the image via editing software, the relative developing process is taking place. In Photoshop, or Corel Paint Shop Pro, etc., one uses the <curves> function to alter the tonal range of a print via; shadow, mid-range and highlight ranges respectively. That is the same as chemically altering the contrast index of a panchromatic negative, and that, is controlled by the D LogE curve which is controlled by developing chemistry and time of development. Even for digital photographers, understanding the black and white "negative" or RAW digital image, is essential in understanding the basic treatment of the image, and outcomes. This subject will be covered specifically in the books on hand coated processes, respectively.

The task of this book is simply to offer an easy to refer to book for developing principles of the black and white negative, chemical principles, and formula basics and applications. I've also included a section on weights and measure conversions, chemical listings with gram to standard measurement standards, with negative and print formulas and processing times for easy access.

I will also cover the basics of black and white metering and Zone System theory, as applied to metering and development, for matching a negative to a print paper or print processing technique, such as a Salted Silver contact print. Understanding the basics of the craft gives the photographer a full set of tools which allow a wide range of options to be used to arrive at the desired look of the final print.

I don't want this book to be a textbook. That is not only no fun at all, but needn't be in order to offer practical insights into the art of black and white photography. There is as much intuition and unique artistic approach to the craft as scientific methodology. This book is written as a guide, to hopefully add dimension to the subject more than a teaching tool. If you practice black and white photography you already know something about it. My intention is to possibly add to that body of knowledge.

This book begins the "Alchemist's Guide; series. This book on b&w film and photo chemistry. That is the intent. So, let's have some fun.

The Black & White Negative

The very beginning to understanding black and white photography is knowing the characteristics of the negative, which \is the basis for everything that comes after you click the shutter. There are three basic areas, or components affecting the negative which will shape the outcome of the finished negative: placing the shot [shoot for the shadows], developer used, and development time.

First, the film type of the negative. The film choice sets the speed and grain structure; however, grain is less visible in today's new T-grain films than in the older films. Speed and grain remain part of the calculous however. Choosing an ISO in today's film selections includes; 100/125 ISO, 200 ISo, 400 ISO, and super speeds of 800 & 1600 press films. Most black and white photographers I know shoot mostly the slower, finer grain films, unless they need speed for movement, then 400 ISO works quite well.

What is important is understanding what film is and how it works. Over the course of this section the characteristics of film will be explained, as well as how those characteristics are seen and measured. First, the negative. The negative is the basis of the photographic printing process, representing the tonalities of the finished print with the reciprocal densities that are the negative form of the positive tonality. Negatives have densities, prints have tonalities.

As can be seen in the simple drawing below, a section of film is viewed from its side. The base layer would be the substratum or the celluloid material that holds the photo emulsion and is hole-keyed on along each edge for winding the film in the camera. The second layer represented in the drawing is the photo sensitive emulsion, in simple terms a gelatin with Silver Halide crystals embedded within. This emulsion, saturated with Silver Halide, will form a latent image when light strikes it, which will create measurable densities in the emulsion upon chemical reduction by a developing agent.

That part of the emulsion that is affected by UV light, begins the Silver Halide transformation into metallic silver, and only that portion, even after chemical development. That portion of the negative that has had no light affect the emulsion, remains unused Silver Halide, as it was, until the film has been rinsed in a bath of Sodium Thiosulfate; Fixer. That fixing bath removes all the unused Silver Halide from the emulsion, permanently removing any light sensitive material that will later affect the finished negative, which now shows clarity, with densities evident.

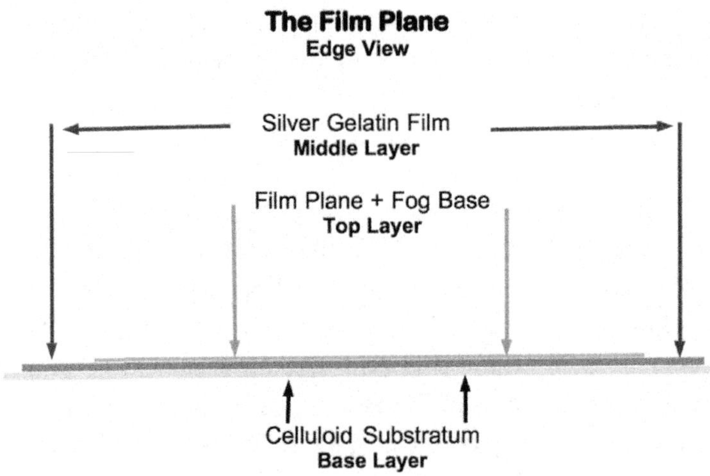

The top layer of the diagram represents the unavoidable fog of the negative emulsion, a film constant. Film Plane + Fog Base; a thin layer of oxidation over the emulsion from coming into contact with air and other elements. There is a very slight 'fogging' on the edge of the emulsion. If you were to take a fresh role of film out of its container, in the dark, then proceed to process the roll as any standard roll, without any light having struck the emulsion, there would remain after development a very thin layer of measurable fog. It is from this measurable edge that begins the real densities on the film plane, measured as tonal ranges.

The variations in film emulsions today continue to offer a wide selection of choices for the black and white photographer. The photographers this book is written for are those that are what I always referred to as Straight Photographers. Those would be photographers who are after the black and white "Fine" print, using standard photographic and darkroom techniques, to arrive at gallery quality prints, most likely on fiber-based papers.

The contents and theories posed in this book derive from that personal experience over the course of many years. It is to those shooters I say, you can be a straight photographer, not relying on bazaar fixes and specialty equipment to have absolute control over your negative, the thing that creates your prints.

The controls over your negative begin with the understanding of how the negative is affected in development, over time. Again the film is seen from a side view, with the emulsion on top the substratum.

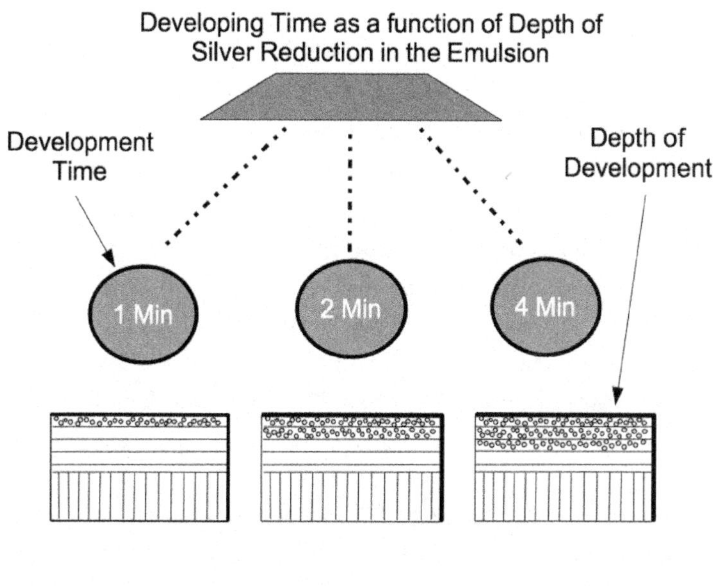

The developing agent must first penetrate the emulsion before the silver reduction process commences. Development proceeds from the surface downwards, ever deeper into the emulsion, over time. All developing agents, or developers, are not equal in their characteristic behavior in this regard. A more aggressive developer will reduce the silver halide more swiftly than a slower working developer, and that tends to harden the emulsion nearer the surface forming a density area before having sufficient time to penetrate to deeper layers of the emulsion.

Reciprocally, a less aggressive developer, usually a fine grain developer or high definition developer, takes more time for penetrating the emulsion and development to occur, thereby reaching deeper into the emulsion to reduce the silver halide embedded there. A major characteristic difference between developers being MQ developers and single developer formulas. MQ developers tend to be much more aggressive developers due to their combined efficiency, or super additivity feature.

The order of this reduction process is more than just emulsion penetration, as the desired intent is reaching deeply into the emulsion to reduce the maximum amount of silver halide to metallic silver as possible. It is the metallic silver that represents your image, it's depth and fullness.

It is also important to understand that the reduction process also moves through the density ranges in order, beginning with zone 1, or first density to show up above *film, plus fog base,* in densitometric terms. As the reducing agent moves deeper into the emulsion, it is also building up the densities of the latent image. After zone 1 has reached it maximum density, zone 2 begins to form, and having reached its maximum density, zone 3 begins to form, with the process continuing until processing is stopped.

With eight identifiable tonal ranges to be represented in the print, there should be eight identifiable density ranges in the negative. There are actually many more tonal ranges represented in the negative than the eight I mention above. Although there will be a long range of densities, there will be eight distinct density ranges that will reciprocally represent the eight tonal ranges of the print.

The first five density ranges of the negative, zone 1-5, or, first and thinnest density up through the fifth density, are reduced in that order, as are all densities. However, it is those first five density ranges that have predetermined density potential. During reduction, as the process moves from the first to the fifth, when each density reaches its maximum density, it cannot be induced to increase in density no matter how much more time is put to it.

Once that developing (reduction) process has moved past zone 5, middle gray, it moves through zone 6, before moving on through zone 7 & 8. These three zones, representing the upper densities of the fuller density range, can be profoundly affected by increasing developing time, or level of *energy* of the developer (reducing agent(s), either by super-additivity or reduction in dilution to a more concentrated form.

It is through understanding these simple principles that the photographer can best utilize these characteristics to their best advantage. Knowing that you can alter your negative by either shortening the tonal range, or expanding it to pretty much any length you wish, within reason, should bring a smile to your face. Those actions of shortening or lengthening the density range, and relative depth of densities is referred to as compactions and expansions, which will be discussed later on.

There are trade-offs in the developing process. Using a more energetic developer, such as an MQ developer, increases energy of the developer, speed of development, and increase densities at the upper end of the density range. Conversely, a compensating developer usually is a slower developer, developing deeper into the emulsion, is a finer grain developer and has more control over the densities in the upper range.

This tradeoff brings up two further characteristics of film & emulsion. Resolution and Acutance.

Resolution:

Resolution is the ability of the emulsion on the film to record very small, fine detail. The size of the silver halide crystals is part of this calculous, with finer grained silver crystals able to record more fine detail than a coarse grain emulsion. This renders the film 'slower' however, from the smaller silver grains being less sensitive to UV light than large ones.

Grain size controls the resolving ability of the emulsion, with the fineness of the grain dictating the smoothness of the tonal range of the picture (in the print), through the fineness of detail. In the final print, resolution, or very fine detail, tends to be prized, for obvious reasons.

High definition developers are basically single reducer formulas that are slower working, as well as a compensating developer. They penetrate more deeply into the emulsion than MQ developers; (Metol/Quinone). During the reduction process high definition, fine grain developers act upon the silver halide crystals differently than MQ developers, keeping them from clustering, which reduces the finer grains for finer detail

Resolution is also controlled by the sharpness or resolving ability of the lens. The resolution of a negative is co-dependent upon three basic elements; film type (grain size), chemical development and the lens used. Using a soft lens will render little negative resolution, even with a fine grain film developed in a high-resolution developer.

Acutance:

Resolution has to do with how small of detail can be represented in the image. Another aspect of film emulsion is the ability to keep the image "sharp". Sharpness has a connection to resolution and fineness of textural detail, however that only goes so far. When a photo is said to be "blurry" it has to do with the edges of objects in the image. More specifically, the edge itself and how many steps or gradations of that edge before becoming defined by another object. When the edges of things in the image are 'soft' or tend to blend into another tone or object edge, we are defining acutance.

Acutance can be defined as the abruptness of the change from one tone (a dark) next to another tone (a light) defined by the edge of each. If that edge drops off quickly from one tone to another it represents high definition; acutance. When the edges of different tones or objects in a photograph are so sharp that it appears, there is a very thin black line along the edges, it is called a Mackie Line. This effect is generally seen between high and low-density edges on the film, leaving a visual effect caused from very high acutance. And a sharp lens.

Resolution then, has to do with fine grains in the emulsion followed by a high-definition or fine grain developer, which has the ability to record very small or fine detail in the scene. Acutance
has to do with the change in density along the line of separation between different tones, or objects in the image. That line of separation has to do with the sharpness of the image, defined by the ability of the developer to keep the edges of different densities of the emulsion short and well defined. Acutance equates to the sharpness of the image.

The high definition is brought about by the way the reduction process acts upon the edges of each tonal range that overlap, being exhausting faster on the denser region, migrating onto the area across the density boundary, accentuating the edges of densities and creating the sharp difference

When talking about photography in general, all films must be included. Even color. This book is focused on black and white photography so I will only mention color this one time. In color film, Gamma is the component one deals with for correct exposure. Gamma is basically controlled by Light Temperature, matched to the film. For daylight film the standard is around 6500 Kelvin temperature. For incandescent lighting the temperature is closer to 3800 Kelvin.

Shooting outside those temperature ranges shifts the Hue of the colors to distort them into something usually hideous. Shooting daylight film indoors under incandescent lighting shifts the color to a sickly yellow. Shooting 'indoor' film balanced for incandescent lighting, outdoors, shifts the color to a deep blue to purple color overall. Both situations shift the temperature outside the color ranges respectively.

In black and white photography, the thing I will deal with is Contrast Index, being the film is panchromatic, and that has to do with densities that represent a tonal range for the print, from black, to white. I will confess here that in older books on the subject, Gamma has been used to refer to the contrast index curve. Very same principles, different nomenclature. I do not do this.

An important part to understand is how the three basic controls of this process works; Shooting choice; placement of shot, developer used and development time. The malleability mentioned earlier has to do with manipulating these variables to arrive at a negative that fits well with the respective tonal range of the print paper to be used. This is what takes the time and experience to realize more fully.

The contrast index curve represents those tonal ranges through their densities, beginning with the toe of the curve, representing the first and thinnest densities of the negative, and extends up through the shoulder of the film's density range, before ultimately curving back down once again, representing an area of natural solarization. Here's an example of the contrast index chart. Next page.

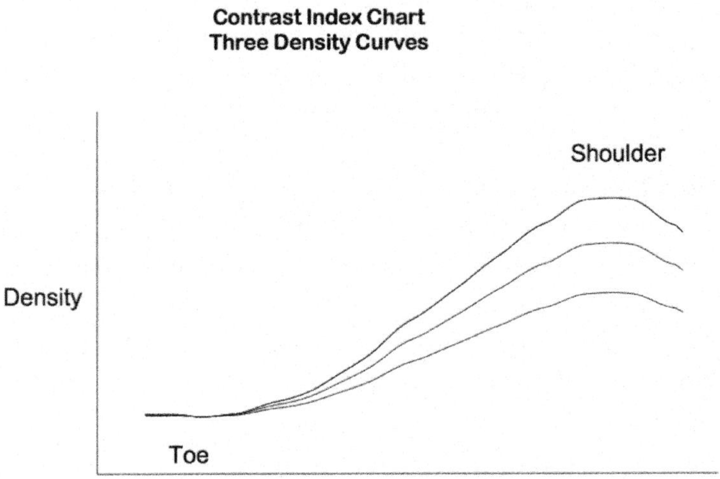

Notice there are three curves in the chart. Each of those curves represents a different contrast index, or, three different outcomes from development. The top line represents the higher contrast range, the lower third line is the flattest and therefore has the longest contrast index range, as measured as middle-tones. It is through the developing process that these curves are controlled.

The truly interesting thing about black and white photography is that there is no hard and fast rule of "correct" shooting or developing. Every variation within the process from clicking the shudder at a given aperture & shutter speed setting, through the various choices of developing, will return a negative with different density characteristics.

Personal taste directs how that is accomplished, and representative of the finished image on the print. The finished print is a tonal reverse-image of the negative. Development of the negative. should be in relation with the printing paper chosen to represent the image. Matching your negative′s tonal range with the paper′s tonal range is very important. Negatives have a far longer tonal range than silver print papers. Negatives can have a range exceeding two-hundred or more, while a good print paper will have maybe fifty. Multi-grade coated stock papers were meant for press, print and journalism printing. Grade rated fiber-based papers were designed for a set range of tones to represent the image. If a photographer knows photo chemistry that isn't a problem.

To realize a fuller understanding of the process from pre-visualization to a finished negative that represents the pre-visualized image, I believe it is absolutely necessary to understand the relationship between metering, chemistry and the basic function of the trademarked Zone System, Ansel Adam's system for dealing with black and the white density scale. and I would say black & white metering. The two are inseparable.

First, it is best to talk about the simple theory of Zone System. For those of you photographers who already understand and use Zone System principles, forgive the rehash here. Many competent photographers don't use the system, or know of it. It is those photographers I encourage to read on.

The fuller theory and application of the Zone System fills a book. That level of familiarity isn't necessary to make it work for you as a black and white photographer. The system works off what you already know. There is a spectrum of grays, from the deepest black, to the brightest of whites, the length of which is the resultant tonal range of the negative, which you control, through chemistry.

The line in the CI chart show a tonal range, as a curve. The bottom of that curve is the *Toe*. At the top where the line begins to curve is the *Shoulder*. The straight portion in between those two points is of course the *straight-line* portion. It is that straight line portion that defines your negative in terms of densities. As the line goes up, the denser that portion of the negative. The Toe is absolute black, the shoulder just sliding into blank white, or paper base white.

As I pointed out earlier, once development goes beyond what the chemical/density represents from the latent image, represented as the area on the other side of the curved shoulder of the CI curve, a natural process of solarization begins. This solarization affects the upper tonal ranges, turning the whites into a dim sooty gray. What is best taken away from this is simply that the mechanical portion of the negative, clicking the shutter, controls, and places the beginning density; [Zone I, absolute black] at the Toe of the CI Curve. That begins the area of interest for printing purposes, which will be discussed later.

One tonal range up, or double the density of Zone I, is Zone II, which represents on the negative, and ultimately the print, the darkest shadow area where it is still black, yet objects inside the shadow area can be made out but do not as yet have any texture, or detail. They are just dark shapes. The zones continue to go up, as densities along the contrast index curve, representing the eight tonal ranges of the theoretical full range print. That curve is logarithmic.

The contrast index curve is simply a line that represents the density scale of the negative. The measurable ability to view the contrast index curve is the D LogE curve function. Interestingly enough, the contrast index cure and the D LogE curve is one and the same. The D LogE curve merely adds the function of density and time to more precisely measure the relationship. It also relies upon the connection to metering, placement of tonal value (pre-visualization) as well as the chemical developer & development time. Using these tools in their natural order and the photographer can know at the time of the shutter release, exactly how the finished print will turn out.

Before viewing the D LogE curve, I believe the correct process is beginning where the first photographic choice sets up the process to the finished print. I'm thinking Silver Gelatin prints for this process. All other processes, using a negative, basically work the same, different formula.

The beginning of this process is observing the object or scene for lighting. Photography is *painting with light.* For this purpose, what you are looking for is zone 3. I'll use the Arabic form for this. That tonal range is in the scene's shadows, where the objects in that shadow range have texture. The viewer of the reciprocal print can make out full texture of the objects viewed. This is the metered value to use in the tonal placement mentioned, and that comes from metering that specific tonal range, separate from the other ranges.

I am of course laying this process out from the practiced perspective of photographing using the field camera, hand held meter method. I'm guessing that method in today's world is the rare breed of shooter. More normally I am speaking to those shooters with DSLR's in hand, or on the tripod. Either way works well, actually I do that too.

I explain this primarily in the mechanically abstract as steps, whereas the importance is devising your own methodology and a practical application that comes of it, as long as it adheres to the known and expected outcomes. DSLR shooters can replicate the steps of the process by simple adaption, in monitoring the subject or scene, selecting the metering for zone 3, clicking the shutter. That begins the process, and by then, only the chemistry can make any changes.

Converting the old-time method of metering and shooting a scene, from field cameras with dark cloths and hand held meters, into modern digital photography would require an application of Edward Weston's practices. There was a hand held meter named the Weston-5, a meter I had once really wanted to have, above my hand-held GE 12° Spot Meter. It was a Weston Meter. It was a prize for believers.

When we metered back then, we walked to the actual place in a scene that we wanted to meter, such as zone 3, took the reading, then wrote it in a day book, under the entry of that day's sheet film listing. We had more time back then. What is important in that form of metering is keeping the extraneous light from interfering. That remains the most accurate form of metering, outside using the Pentax 1° Spot Meter, or equivalent. Specific readings make specific developing plans.

Edward Weston was known to have put down his hand-held meter after some years and instead relied on the palm of his hand, held in the light he wanted to capture in full detail. If his subject was to be in full sunlight, he held his palm out to the full sunlight, if it was to be in shadow he held his palm out in shadow, (turn your back to the sun and read your hand in shade), making his shutter/aperture setting decision on the light quality off the palm of his hand.

That really isn't crazy. The reflective light off the palm of your hand is equivalent to zone 6. That would be roughly the same reading you would get through the EI lens of a DSLR camera when metering the average outdoor scene with the sky in the frame. Zone six. That puts the image on the straight line of the contrast index, and that potentially represents a full range of tones for the print. But that is unpredictable.

Zone 6 is one stop open from zone 5, pushing the tonal range upward towards the shoulder slightly. This increase in overall densities gives better shadow detail than had the image been shot one stop less, which would place the beginning of the tonal range (zone1) at the very toe of the curve. That position of zone 1 as near the toe as possible was the catchword of photography fifty years ago when film was far more saturated with silver halide crystals. Before the advent of T-Grain films.

So what Edward Weston had come to realize was simply that once you know your lighting, your film and chemistry, you are able to make a fine photographic print by developing a negative with just the right amount of lighting, in a formulae that will leave the negative with a perfect tonal range to print on a fiber based paper that will represent the image as he visualized it beforehand. He did this repeatedly.

The only metering information you need to know can be replicated without having to make the quarter mile jaunt we did in the stupid old days to directly measure the light in a shadowed area somewhere in the scene. One need merely turn away from the sun and take a meter reading of the palm of their hand while in the body's shadow, as described above. That is zone six, in a shadow. If you want zone six to show up in the shadow of your scene, then stop down three stops (or speed up the shutter by three settings) and shoot. What you will want to know of course, is how many stops away is zone 7, from this zone 3? That tells you your development time.

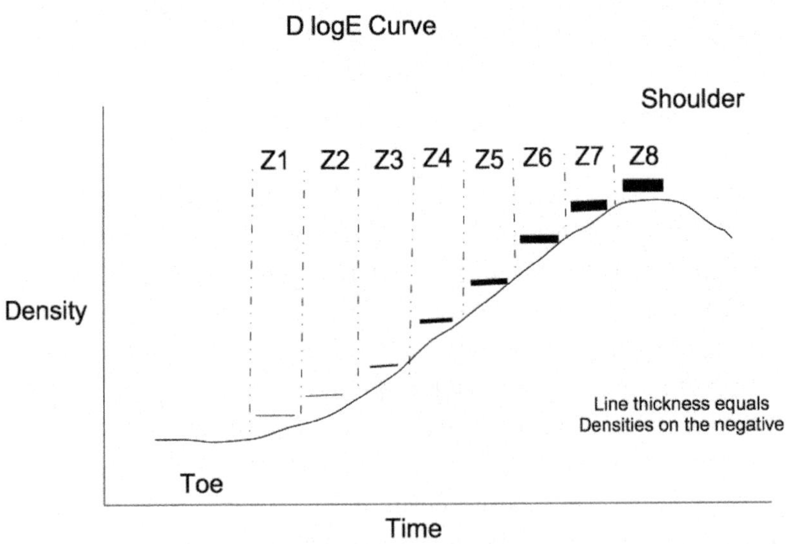

The diagram shows a simple contrast index curve with the added density range of a negative along the slope of the curve. The density range of a negative is the difference in density between zone 1 and zone 7.

The important aspect of this sloped line are the two functions, with segmented lines representing the eight zone ranges and reciprocal negative densities representing each zone range. These two intertwined relationships become the crux of understanding the principle of the metered placement of the zone 3 tonal value when shooting, and chemical development decisions for that negative, or roll of film. This is the procedure to arrive at the best printable image in the printing phase.

Study of the D LogE curve will show the relationship of a given theoretical zone, such as zone 1, with a measurable density. That density, read via a densitometer, will show the given density just above the density of the negative's *film base plus fog*. That density, on a final print, will show absolute black, or as black as the paper's silver content is capable of rendering. Each zone forward, with the reciprocal increased negative density, represents roughly doubling the measurable density of the previous density. A logarithmic relationship.

Utilizing the ability to place a tonal area (zone) at a given spot when shooting, allows the photographer the ability to structure the tonal scale in a scene or of a subject, when applying this portion of the process with a reciprocal developing strategy that compliments the strategy by producing the desired tonal relationship as pre-visualized. The shutter of the camera controls the overall placement of the image's potential tonal scale, permanently fixing the position of the first five zones, or tonal densities, even after development. The chemical developing controls the overall development of the negative, affecting mostly the upper three tonal ranges of the negative; zone 6, 7, & 8, respectively.

No amount of development can alter the bottom five densities once they have been set by the click of the shutter. There is some argument over whether zone 5 is altered by extended development, however, my experience is that for the most part, zone 5 is little unchanged by the time zone 6 becomes part of the picture.

As a rehash then, when metering for a scene, the most important element to meter is a reflective metering of zone 3, or that area of the image that represents a shadowed area where the photographer wants the objects therein to have texture. The meter reading will read that value as middle gray, (zone 5), thus, the photographer then stops down the shutter two stops, or speeds up the shutter speed setting by two to represent that metered zone.

When the photographer *places* their shot at zone 3, that merely sets up the overall tonal range to lie on the straight line of the contrast index curve, where the image's tonal range is optimal for separation of tonal values, and therefore a full range print. The other half of that calculous is the developing of that negative image to insure that the full tonal range is indeed represented.

The other half of the metering process is identifying the second textural zone of the image, (zone 7). This textural zone identifies the area in the scene that is white, where the photographer wants to retain the texture in that tonal range. Knowing the value of this zone, or tonal range, identifies the amount of developing time necessary for achieving the full tonal range of the scene, as pre-visualized. Development controls the upper densities, and the length of the overall tonal range.

Not all scenes, or subjects need be a full eight tonal range image. There are times when a photography desires a softer, flatter image, for the effect they want. There are times when the scene is very contrasty, in full sun, when the photographer wants to show detail in the shadowed areas. Placement of a tonal value in these situations is critical to achieve either objective.

The developing methods controlling these two situations are expansions and compactions, respectively. These two actions are accomplished by altering the developing time, and/or developer, to control the tonal range of any given negative. These two methods will be discussed in further detail in the section on development and formulas.

All the above discussion on the negative and placement of value does have a point, eventually. But the real point being that shooting the scene, or subject, is only half the story. The thing that controls the ultimate image on the negative is the developing process, and the developer that does the work. Understanding photo chemistry is the best way to have any conceivable control over the photographic image.

Before dealing with the chemistry and formulas, it is important to understand the relationship between the mechanical part of photography and the secondary chemical partner. The mechanical part is camera settings. The chemical part comes later, reducing the latent image on the negative to a predictable density range, that will ultimately make the desired metallic silver print. Making the optimal camera setting has to do with metering, and tone placement. Understanding what the optimal setting might be, is learned firsthand from a texture test. That comes next, in Part II; the controls of the negative.

Controlling the Negative

Texture Tests:

The above discussion on contrast index curves and densities on a negative are theoretical explanations to the practical application of the process. Understanding the relationship between zone placement when shooting, followed by chemical development of the negative is important. What is equally important is a simple shooting test to know exactly how that procedure will actually turn out.

Every lens you use is unique, and will give slightly different results from other lenses keeping all else unchanged. Developers and developing times will certainly alter the density outcomes of a negative. It is for this reason every serious black and white photographer do a simple texture test for their equipment and chosen developer.

The test is simple. Take a white, textured bath towel, laying it flat on a hard surface, in even light. North light works fine for this, as it is daylight, with no tonal value shifts from other lighting sources. Set up the camera as if you are doing copy work, with the camera straight on, 90 degrees to the towel surface, close enough to fill the lens with towel surface.

Meter the towel. That will return a value, aperture & shutter speed, which is an averaged middle gray. You want the first density to show up on the film plane as zone 1. Absolute black. To make that happen, stop down four stops. From zone 5; middle gray, to zone 1; four stops down. Take the first shot.

Now open the lens one stop; shoot again. Open another stop and shoot, and continue on, opening one stop each time until you have ten stepped shots. You now have a theoretical range of densities representing the latent image. For now, we leave the developing to formula X, which you will use to develop those ten images on that roll of film. For format camera shooters using sheet film I will include a procedure to make simple cut film holder slides to do this test on one sheet of film; in the appendix section.

When you develop that strip of film, you will see ten distinct tonal ranges. What you will be choosing, is that thinnest tonal range that is absolute black, *two stops from the tonal range that just begins to show texture in the frame.* That would be two stops down from zone 3, the first textural density of the negative, and reciprocal tonal range on the contrast index cure.

What you know from this test is how many stops down you will want to go after metering for zone 3, when you shoot, and secondly, how long you want to develop to achieve a full eight tonal ranges, ending up with a non-textured white, with a textured white one stop down. You will be controlling the tonal range, as well as where it will be on the contrast index curve. There was a time when I used this test to move my contrast index up near the shoulder, to show more shadow detail in the print. Anyone familiar with W. Eugene Smith knows he shot his images right from the base of the toe, giving a more dramatic, theatrical feel with his lighting. The choice is yours.

The towel test offers the photographer a preview of the real effects of metering and development of the chosen film. Lower ISO rated films will have a slightly steeper contrast index than faster ISO ratings, as well as less grain. The 400 ISO films will have a longer tonal range on average, keeping developing constant, a reciprocal of the lower contrast index curve.

The second portion of this test is the development of the negatives. For now that is a constant. Later, in the photo chemical section, you will see how to alter the values on the D logE curve by altering the formulas for the developers, and time of development. Along with the concepts of compaction and expansion of the tonal range. The towel texture test, in my experience, is absolutely essential for knowing how your photograph is going to turn out. For that to happen, the metering and zone placement have to be known, as well as developing formula and development time afterwards. Those are the photographer's tools.

Metering:

Before I get derided for bringing up metering to a sophisticated reader, it should be known that, truth be told, most shooters today do not place their shot based upon the metered reading of zone 3. I rest my case.

Today, EI metering is what happens when you "see" your shot through the lens of the camera, and what is actually being metered, is the *average* of the total light range of the subject area. Also remember, black and white metering has to do with *reflective* metering, not ambient light metering as done with color. Take your meter reading from the reflection of an object to the meter.

That, in today's DSLR, through the lens sampling, deduces to an average within the range of zone 6, although the meter reads middle gray, as the it is seeking out the middle detail and favors the sky, when it is included. Otherwise, it will tend to push the lighting range into the higher portion of the CI curve in order to preserve shadow detail.

As I said, it's theoretical in nature, yet easy to understand, once you begin. Theoretically, when you are looking at a scene, which, for this purpose works best as it will include all eight tonal zones of the fuller range. I used a hand held GE photo-voltaic meter with a closed lid 12-degree metering view. Open lid increased the view angle and sensitivity. What was important was getting a direct reading on the two tonal ranges, zone values, that define the CI curve, D LogE curve, and ultimately the densities on the negative. Those two zones are zone 3, and zone 7. Those are the two *Textural* zones.

Zone 3 has already been described above. A shadow with objects that have full texture. Zone 7 is at the other end of the tonal range near the top of the curve, representing the whites. Zone 7 is white, with full texture on objects within that range. The zone above that is zone 8, which is pure white, no texture; paper base white for printing.

Shooting the scene, clicking the shutter, controls the low end of the negative; zone 1 through zone 5. Chemistry controls the upper end of the tonal ranges; zone 6 through zone 8. Shoot for zone 3 and develop for zone 8. You're shooting for shadow details and developing for highlights. More on that in the section on developing.

So, metering with a DSLR, hopefully with a zoom lens one can poke the lens entirely into a shadowed area, or, the old-fashioned way of actually walking over to the shadowed area and sticking the camera within, to take a meter reading, then of course noting that in the photo journal or day book you carry with you, for such notations and notes on a shot; for later. Then trudge back to the camera position for shooting.

Now, in your little book you can map out the zone metering and begin making the setting adjustments, by taking a second reading on that object that would be white in the scene, yet still have at least some visual detail. That's of course zone 7, and you need to know what that reading is to make the choice for development time. If you don't know what zone 7 is you really don't know how long to develop the negative for the expected full tonal range (on the print) of eight distinct tonal ranges.

All metering, ALL metering no matter the meter, is middle grey; 18% reflective gray. That is all a light meter is capable of doing, evaluating light. When you meter anything you are reading Zone 5 *in that light range.* If you stick your metering device into a zone 3 (shadow) you are still reading middle gray for that light range. To have that reading to show up in the negative as a zone 3 shadow area, you convert the middle gray setting, to the zone 3 setting, or, set your camera two steps down. You either close down two apertures, or increase the shutter speed by two settings. Either action sets the scene according to zone 3, shadow detail.

The next metered area, really *surface,* is zone 7. Find the white area of the scene where you want some texture, not pure white. Pure white, or blank white, is paper base white, not color at all. Meter the zone 7 area, or that white which has some texture, then note that in your book. That reading should be four stops higher than the recording for zone 3. That tells you that there is a standard 5-stop lighting spread, which is typical for an average sunny day. That means standard developing time.

As seen in the chart of negative densities, is the progression of densities from zone 1 [dMax black] all the way through zone 7, the textured white and thickest density. The relationship between these densities is logarithmic, with each density twice that of the preceding one, or, double the units of light for each proceeding density. The importance of this relationship has to do with matching the contrast index tonal values to the paper for which you will be printing on. Negatives have approximately 250 potential tonalities. Fiber based printing papers have approximately 50. This relationship is important.

What it looks like on a chart:

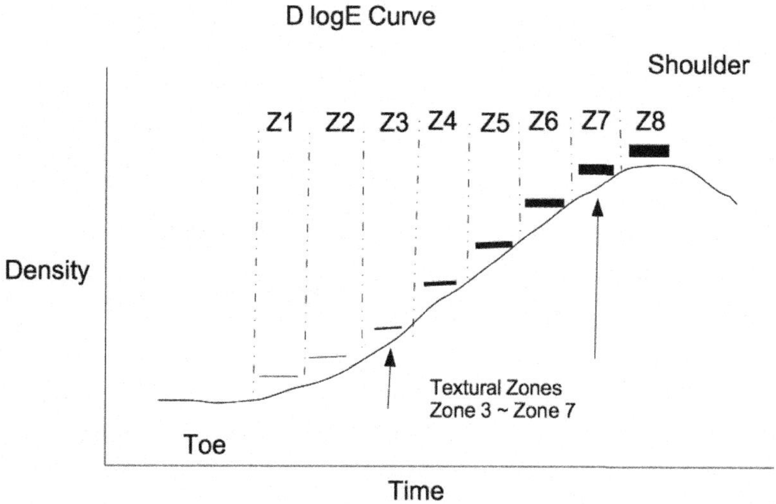

Notice the thinner densities at the bottom near the toe, with each subsequent density thicker as it moves up the curve towards the shoulder. These densities represent the eight distinct densities of the full tonal range. Z1 thru Z5 are the densities that are fixed. Z6 thru Z8 are the densities that can be profoundly affected by development.

Those two metered spots tell you at what setting to shoot the scene, and the time needed for development, for the selected developer. Each developer may have a different concentration and developing time, based upon the tests you performed before ever going out to photograph.

Taking the abstract discussion of metering and texture tests into concrete analysis is achieved best by viewing it all on paper. The D logE curve here shows the same density ranges along the contrast index curve with the focus now on two densities. These are the two densities to be metered in any scene. These are the two values that identify the characteristic and range of the resultant negative image. The lower density, zone 3, sets the value for which the camera setting is determined, as aperture

& shutter speed. That sets up the point at which the first tonal density will show up on the film plane, as zone 1.

The second tonal density, or zone, to be metered and recorded is zone 7, that white area that you still want to show texture and detail. That tells the photographer what is needed in development to realize the tonal range desired, which is up to the photographer to decide. From the texture test of your negative, the actual tonal range is known, from the developer and developing time used in processing that negative or roll of film. That is why the texture text is desirable.

So, to recap. Identifying the camera setting for a scene is achieved through metering two identified zones; zone 3, or that area of a scene that is in shadows, that you want texture and detail of objects, and zone 7, or the white surfaces in the scene where you want to retain texture and detail. Those two readings tell you everything you need to know about the light composition of the scene to be photographed and the given tonal range of your negative. The task of manipulating the given tonal range of a negative image, to achieve a different tonal range, has to do with manipulating the developing formula, and development times, and that is photo chemistry.

To be fair to the larger arena of photographers of today, digital imagery is all you know, and your work lies within the available software at hand. Understanding the black and white image as a process continues to be valuable, as the principles of black and white photography remain the same, with variations in the process application. Contrast index remains the same, and the controls of processing change from chemical to algorithmic, but the end result remains unchanged.

To alter the contrast index of a black and white negative, is achieved through chemistry, by altering the developing formula or its dilution, or altering the time of development. However, without also altering the placement of tonal values before shooting, the chemistry only affects those tonal densities after zone 5, or middle gray. Chemical development controls the highlights, which are represented by the top three tonal densities; zone 6, 7, and 8.

To alter the contrast index of a black and white digital negative image, one employs the digital tool equivalent of the Curve function in the tool menu. The curve function is a digital contrast index line curve. One clicks on any point along that curve to anchor that point, which keeps that part of the line from moving. The change to the curved line is accomplished by clicking on the line and moving the line either up or down, thereby altering the amount of theoretical light that represents that part of the curve. The image preview allows one to see the darkening and lightening of the image as the line is shifted from its original position.

Anchor points can be made to identify a section of the negative that is desired to be lightened, without affect any other portion of the image. The same for darkening a portion of the image, say deepening blacks, by anchoring above the toe around zone 2, then lowering the graph line. The same can be done on the highlights by anchoring a point near the shoulder of the curve then raising the top portion of the curve to increase the brightness of the whites.

Digital manipulation of digital imagery is an art form, no different than chemical manipulation of a black and white negative. Different tools for different mediums, both however, functionally doing the same task. I have no practical advice for digital manipulation other than to say, find a good book on digital photographic techniques.

In digital photography, one can deepen blacks and shadowed areas by moving the curved line downward, using software. In film, the photographer achieves that by placing their metered zone 3 reading one range lower, (stop down three stops instead of two) moving the beginning of the CI curve lower, closer to the toe. There will be less densities at the lower end, resulting in deeper blacks and less shadow detail in the finished print. That can offer a more dramatic appeal to the finished image in some cases.

Another means of adjusting the position of densities on the straight line of the contrast index curve is by altering the ISO. As I've mentioned, I preferred shooting near the shoulder. My method was to set my ISO rated 100/125 film to ISO 80. This is theoretically "overexposing" the film, which I controlled by using a single reducer fine grain compensating developer to control the densities representing the highlights. To know to what extent, I needed to so this, I used a texture text.

This method also allows for lowering the threshold density towards the toe by rating the same ISO 100/125 film to ISO 160. This moves the range of densities on the contrast index curve downward towards the tow, reducing the amount of texture in the lower density ranges.

As I've made clear, repeatedly, the focus of this book is for black and white photographers interested in having the fullest control over their negatives, their images, which is an art form that combines shooting and developing. Those two processes, when effectively combined, give the photographer completely predictable results with consistency, over time. It is this commitment to a combined application that makes every difference in the final image.

Now it's time for photo chemistry.

Black & White Photo Chemistry

The Chemical Trail

Black and white photo chemistry can be very complex, filled with mathematical principles and formulae theories that can be a real thrill killer. But then again, you don't need to be a PhD in chemistry to understand how it applies to your black and white negative. Photo chemistry is only as hard as you make it, and how deep you want to wade into the subject.

My intention is to offer a fuller explanation of a process that controls the characteristics of the negative you are processing, without it becoming a textbook. This book is a guide to be used to learn the principles that shape and control your finished negatives. All the preceding material was but the setup to understanding the material to come. The preceding material has to do with preparing the negative for processing. At this point, the photographer will have a latent image on the negative in hand, ready to develop.

The texture text is for the developer you plan on using during normal development of your negatives. That is why you are doing the test, to see what affect that developer has on your choice of tone placement after metering the scene. The results are right there on that roll of film, or single sheet film. That assumes you are competent to *read* the negative for correct densities, or have printed a proof sheet of the negatives to see the final outcome in print.

Speaking about the chemical characteristics of black and white photo chemistry is not unlike speaking about the culinary skill of baking, and the makeup of baking recipes. In both instances there are basic constituent ingredients, which work together to become a predictable outcome. Each constituent ingredient has known characteristics, as well as known outcomes from being mixed with other constituents.

In baking, common dry ingredients would be flour, salt, sugar, baking powder and sometimes one or two others, to arrive at different baked goods, pancakes, pies, cakes, puff pastries or pizza. By altering the recipe, one alters the outcome in known ways. Pre-visualizing a scene with metering and zone placement, followed by chemical reduction of the latent image is no different in principle. There are formulas that will work with any conceivable condition, to arrive at the image as pre-conceived.

Principles of a Formula:

The makeup of a developer is based upon three primary functions of any given photographic formula. Technically, there is a fourth; the restrainer. However, being I do not use the traditional restrainer in the formulas listed in this book, I take the restrainer out of the discussion for now. The three chemical constituents used in this book will be reducer, preservative, and accelerator. The fourth element, the restrainer, I will cover in the chemical section, as it should be understood, and why it is utilized, when it is.

The reducing agent can be one or more chemical ingredients. There is also the consideration in the differences between negative development and print development. The former usually requiring stronger mixtures than the latter. Also the formulas for both type of development differ in their tasks, respectively.

From my own experiences in developing, I have found that using Metol alone in negative development brings about the best results, while print development was best served by using both reducing agents, albeit at times, in separate developing baths, which I will cover more fully later on.

Reading most analysis of developers these days would imply that using Metol alone is not the norm, that adding the second reducer, Hydroquinone, is recommended. Perhaps for convenience, using a pre-packaged developer such as D-76, might be a valid point. However, I have found two developers without any Hydroquinone that are superior to M/Q developers, in fine grain properties, control of upper tonal densities for retaining textural detail, easy and cheap to use, and having long shelf life. I will be making a big deal out of both those developers in the formula section of this chapter.

Each reducing agent has its own characteristics when it comes to developing energy, working longevity, contrast outcomes and granularity issues. When used alone, each keeps within these limitations. When two reducing agents are used in combination, there is an effect called 'super-additivity', which shows an exponential outcome of reduction properties; as far more development energy, higher contrast and shorter developing times. Super-additivity is the Gestalt Effect, being the combination of elements exceeds the sum of their respective parts, used alone. The most common of this example is Metol & Hydroquinone.

Metol acts more immediately on the image, is long lasting, but of low contrast, especially on the print. Hydroquinone takes longer to act upon the image but when it does the action on the image is swift, again, especially on the print. When these two reducers are added together, in concert they are swift acting, long lasting and energetic, with the ability to modulate the affects by simply reducing or increasing the amounts of each reducer, respectively, in the formula.

I will cover the basics of the constituent chemical agents that will be used for almost all development of the negative and finished print, covered in this book. They will be divided into the three primary categories mentioned above; reducer, preserver and accelerator.

High definition developing is an outcome most photographers strive for. High definition developing is another way of describing negatives with enhanced acutance that conversely makes prints with good image sharpness. High acutance with good texture and detail in a separated tonal range.

The newer T-grain films of today are of a fine, thin emulsion, and used in conjunction with a pre-packaged MQ developer, with a tendency for a more contrasty negative, therefore formulas that work to control excessive contrast are preferred. These developers also tend to be fine grain developers, and tend to fall under the heading of *compensating developers*.

Controlling for excessive contrast is one portion of the formula, the other portion is seeing to it that the fuller gradation of tonal ranges must not suffer. There need be a full tonal density range representing the full reflective range of the original scene. Those requirements can be satisfied by using a single developing agent (Metol) which is a low energy (soft-working) developer, which, working on its own, allows it to become exhausted rapidly in the denser portions of the negative.

This diluted developer in the above reduction process would not develop the shadow details fully, nor be able to continue the reducing process for long, without a high alkali content to work with the reducer. This combination of low energy developer in conjunction with high alkalinity formulas are known for high definition, fine grain compensating developers.

The process by which high definition developers work goes something like this. The active developing agent reduces the silver halide at different rates on the negative, exhausting itself sooner in the denser areas with the most silver halide concentration. The developer in the lighter area migrates over the edge into the denser portion, as the developer there becomes exhausted, with the developer in the darker region then migrating over the edge retarding development on that side the edge. That combination of the developer migrating from one density to another at their border edges constitutes the resultant edge referred to as *acutance, or sharpness*.

This effect can also be enhanced with high acutance developers, which will be displayed below. These formulas are single developers, some relying on accelerators and others working in their simplest form of reducer in high alkalinity alone. As you look through the formulas, make note of the constituent chemical elements, their respective quantities, or absence. These formulas are very well suited for shooting conditions in the southwestern United States. That is because the spectral light quality is shifted to the red, which makes compensating developers a photographer's best friend.

SECTION 1
Chemical Constituents

Reducers:
Metol;
Methyl-paraminophenol sulphate

There are two reducing chemicals still used regularly for development; Metol (Elon), and Hydroquinone. There is also Phenidone, but that is not regularly used. What can be said about Metol is that it is a slower working reducer that continues to work over time. It is only slightly affected by temperature during use and is soluble and easily mixed in water.

Metol alone, as a developer, works with both alkaline agents of sodium or potassium carbonates. Used together Metol and one of the carbonates makes a energetic developer, with control over the contrast of the negative regulated by dilution of the developer. Metol used solely with sodium sulfite alone also makes excellent working fine grain developer, which can be regulated for more energetic development and negative contrast by using a more concentrated mixture. There is a fairly wide range of workable solutions to developing needs by altering the formula as needed.

At one time, impurities in Metol gave it a bad reputation for a type of skin poisoning, or dermatitis condition, but in modern use that problem has been erased. One other reducing agent was used as a substitute; Phenidone (reducer). Today's Metol no longer has any impurities as before. In short, Metol is a very good developer for negative development when used alone, and has a very good shelf life.

Metol is also used in print developing, used most often in conjunction with hydroquinone in single bath formulas. Metol can also be effectively used separately, but in union with hydroquinone, in a split bath printing formula. For me, the split bath method was most effective in separating and controlling the tonal scale during development.

Hydroquinone;
Para-dihydroxy benzene

Hydroquinone is a reducing agent that is fairly soluble in cold water and easily soluble in warm water, with is the preferred mixing temperature for most developers being 110° F. Hydroquinone can be used alone as a reducer for certain processes, like high contrast negatives for commercial purposes. When used with alkali carbonates it is a slow working, but contrasty developer. When used with a caustic alkalies, such as sodium hydroxide, it becomes a very energetic developer giving the highest possible contrast range.

Hydroquinone is also a mainstay print developer as well and is usually paired with Metol for most formulas, however I will be focusing on a split bath development procedure that allows direct visual inspection of each reducer as it affects the print during processing. The expression of *super additivity* is descriptive of these two reducing agents being combined. Metol & Hydroquinone is likely the most widely used developer formula today. It is the basis of Kodak's D-76 negative developer, and their Dektol paper developer.

Pyrocatechin; Catechol
Ortho-dihydroxy benzene

Pyrocatechin is a reducing agent closely related to Hydroquinone, although there are some distinct differences as well. Pyrocatechin, usually referred to as Pyro, is not to be confused with its cousin Pyrogallic acid, another Pyro. This form is liquid and is a staining developer, on the negatives and fingers. It is highly susceptible to oxidation and keeps poorly. Like Pyrocatechin, it is a tanning agent.

Pyro(catechin) is easily soluble in warm water, and as noted it is a tanning agent, with the amount of tanning quality dependent of the level of sulfite used in the formula. The less sulfite, the more reciprocal tanning of the negative, equal to the increase in density. This tanning is in the form is altering the color of the negative from traditional black, to a soft transparent brown. Although the densities on a tanned negative appear thinner than standard black colored densities, they are not.

Pyro can be combined with sodium or potassium carbonate as the accelerator giving sharp detail and long tonal range. However, it is when used in conjunction with a caustic alkali that it becomes not only a very energetic developer, but the resultant acutance of the negative is unsurpassed. Running your finger over the emulsion side of such a developed negative feel like a Bah Relief.

There will be more discussion on this developing agent as well as formulas for its use, with the focus being on acutance and high definition. Understanding basic characteristics of the developing agents is important in deciding the type of developer that would most benefit your photography. There is one formula that in my mind out shines all the rest. It is easily mixed, cheap, has a very long shelf life, and has the best all-around developing qualities one could ask for. There will be ample fanfare when I introduce it later on.

Alternative Reducers/Developers:
Phenidone;

There are other developers, or reducing agents that can be employed, like Phenidone, Amidol or Rodinal, all of which have their specific application and signature characteristics. Phenidone, as mentioned earlier is very similar to Metol, although a more potent form, needing much less by weight than Metol to equal the equivalent developing action. Phenidone not only works in conjunction with Hydroquinone, creating the 'super additivity' effect, but Hydroquinone effectively reacts with the oxidized elements to reform Phenidone. Phenidone's developing properties are dependent on the pH of developing solution like any other developer, but unlike some developers, Phenidone's developing activity increased with the increase in pH.

I can only speculate on why Phenidone has not become a more mainstream developing agent. Although it is more expensive than Metol, the amounts used in a formula, compared to Metol, is so much less that it is actually cheaper to use. It is also known to be the go-to developer when Metol or other reducers brought about skin reactions like dermatitis.

Although Phenidone was first discovered in 1890, it wasn't made commercially available until the 1950's, and by then other developers had become the standard.

Rodinal;

I will mention Rodinal as I have used it on a few occasions to observe first-hand the unique characteristics as a developer. Rodinal is not a fine grain developer, although it is known for it's acutance on the negative. Rodinal works without the repeated or continual agitation of the negative during development as other developing agents require for even development.

It works most vigorously on the dark portions of the negative, and when that area overlaps a lighter area that action creates the high acutance along the edge of the variant tonal ranges. Rodinal is also known to alter the deeper blacks identified around shadow detail and lower tonal ranges, leaving density alignments that give the final image softer blacks with more shadow detail, a less contrasty image, and a more warmed toned effect in the print.

The times I utilized Rodinal as a developer was in conjunction with 6cm x 9cm negatives from a Century Graflex camera I used before moving into a Burke & James 5x7 flatbed camera. I used ISO 125 rated sheet film (ASA) rated at the time, so negative grain was not a primary concern. One of the images I shot was a handmade wooden bath-house, one of the buildings at a commune outside Eugene, Oregon. Butler Green. The end result of the Rodinal development rendered the raw wood of the building in great detail, highlighting the texture of the wood very well. The shadow details in the print were enhanced, showing more texture and detail on the surfaces within the shadowed area.

At that time, sheet film was available in ASA 50, which as mentioned earlier would have a higher contrast index than a film with higher sensitivity rating; 125, 250, 400 respectively. Rodinal works quite well with such a film because it enhances the low and high tonal range differences in the form of acutance, as well as keeps the shadow detail that might normally get lost in developing with an M/Q (Metol/Hydroquinone) developer.

Rodinal is used in very diluted solutions. They can range from 1:20, 1:50 or even 1:100 dilutions, for long periods of time, compared to other developers. For those photographers who tend to seek alternative methods to realize unique enhancement of their photographs, Rodinal is worth exploring. Rodinal negatives work well for enlargement printing or contact printing.

Amidol;
2, 4-diaminophenol dihydrochloride

Amidol has been around since 1890, as have other chemical reducing agents. It has its quirks as well as stated advantages for the printing process. Amidol is poisonous and stains much of what it comes into contact with. The staining property of Amidol is due to its oxidation when in contact with air, from the free base of Amidol when in a neutral or a solution form. Using tongs or rubber gloves when developing is highly advised.

Amidol gets much of its notoriety and fame from Edward Weston's religious use of it as his primary print developer. It is known to render deep blacks and crisp whites. Soft, high-key prints are also very desirable for this print developer, which can be used in highly diluted form and still render beautiful detail. As also known about Edward Weston's love affair with Amidol, he was known to have had stained fingers from developing his prints with this chemical reducer. That doesn't thwart its use by fine art printers who continue to revere this developer.

Preservative:
Sodium Sulfite;

A preservative element in the reduction process comes into play to control the natural oxidation process of the reducer. As the reducer works on the silver halide emulsion, oxidation from the chemical reduction increases over time, thereby reducing the effectiveness of overall reduction. Simply put, the development of the negative becomes hindered by oxidation and the fuller latent image wouldn't get reduced/developed without the aid of a preservative element, such as sodium sulfite.

This principle of chemical exhaustion also comes into play during development if no agitation is used during processing. The chemical solution of the reducer, in contact with the negative emulsion becomes depleted over time, in those areas specific to higher levels of the silver halide. Without continuous or at least timed intervals of agitation of the negative in solution, the resultant negative image would be much flatter and far less desirable.

Sodium sulfite then, preserves the reduction process over time, allowing continuous reduction of the silver halide crystals to their metallic silver form to the fullest of the developing agent's ability. Notice I use the terms reducer and developer interchangeably. For all practical purposes, they are one and the same.

Sodium sulfite can also become an accelerator, even a reducing agent in high enough concentrations. I will be highlighting two such respective formulas using sodium sulfite to also act as an accelerator, and a formula that uses it for increasing reduction, later. For now it should be known that the pH of the alkali element increases the reduction process, speeding up development and increasing contrast. That is why caustic alkalis such as sodium hydroxide tend to be high-energy developers. They are also known as high-definition and high acutance developers, although not fine grain developers, although that can be overcome.

Sodium sulfite is the most commonly used preservative for developing, both negative and film. It is versatile, keeps well in dry conditions, is easy to procure and is relatively inexpensive when compared to other constituent chemicals. The Photographer's Formulary is one good place to find photo-chemicals in bulk. Sodium sulfite is in all the formulas I have come across, and have used myself, which will be represented in this book, so I will refrain going into other possible preservatives, although they exist.

Accelerators:
Sodium Carbonate;
Anhydrous (concentrated) & Monohydrate (more water)
washing soda, soda ash, soda crystals

Sodium Carbonate is another basic element of developing formulas for negatives and prints. Sodium carbonate is an alkali, which is necessary for the reducing agents to actuate their chemical properties on the emulsion. Alkaline's are measured and rated for their pH level, with the higher the pH level the more energetic the development, as well as increase in the halide grain size. The lower the pH level the smaller the grain size.

Sodium carbonate has a pH value of approximately 11.5-11.6, which is relatively high considering Borax, another alkali has a pH value of 9.5 and is considered part of fine grain developers. For calculation purposes, sodium carbonate is 100 times as alkaline as Borax. The pH scale is also logarithmic. An even higher alkaline rated accelerator is sodium hydroxide with a pH value of 12-14. Sodium Hydroxide (Na OH) is likely the most volatile chemical used in standard photographic development. A small amount added to room temperature water in a flask can make the water boil. Never, ever add water onto otherwise dry sodium hydroxide. It would basically explode into wet fireworks.

Potassium Carbonate:
Anhydrous (concentrated) & Monohydrate (more water)
Pearl-ash, Potash, PotCarb

Potassium Carbonate is another alkaline accelerator used in photo development. Potassium carbonate is of a higher pH alkaline value than sodium carbonate in its anhydrous form. Most formulas I have come across have sodium carbonate as the accelerator. What I have come to find from experience is that using potassium carbonate shifts the tonal structure in a subtle way, tending to cool the image in the printed form, whereas sodium carbonate tends to warm the print tones. I have no explanation for this shift, although there may very well be an excellent reason identified on a photographer's forum for those needing such explanations.

Should you look over the chemical properties of the constituent elements in the final section of this book, you would see the comparison of $Na_2 CO_3.10H_2O$ (sodium carbonate) and $K_2 CO_3$ (potassium carbonate), with the sodium form taking a bit less by volume to equal the potassium form, both being in anhydrous powders. The anhydrous form of a chemical is a more concentrated form, from less water in the final compound. It takes more, by weight, of a chemical compound in dehydrated form in a mixture, than in anhydrous form. There is a conversion table in Part 5 that shows this conversion for usE in formulas, using one form to another. The developing results, in densities, don't change from using either form.

Restrainer:
Potassium Bromide:
K Br

During the chemical reduction process, the action of the reducing agent on the emulsion brings about a natural oxidation process as a byproduct of the chemical reduction. The fuller description of that process could be a chapter for chemistry students. What you need to know about that process is that oxidation during the reduction process equals fog on the film. That is an undesirable outcome of the development process.

It is the preservative in the formula (sodium sulfite) that keeps the same oxidation process, an outcome of the reducing agent on the emulsion, from slowing or stopping the developing action. It is the restraining agent that keeps the oxidation from creating fog on the emulsion. The go-to chemical as a restrainer is potassium bromide.

Many of the developing formulas that include potassium bromide generally show it in gram weight, like the other constituents in the formula. It is also the last to be added to the developing solution, and is listed last in the formula. Potassium bromide is easily soluble in water, and stores well in diluted solution. I have found that making a 10% solution of the potassium bromide, then adding to the formula in milliliter form. You know from Part 5: equivalents, that 10ml's of 10% solution equals 1 gram.

There are numerous developer formulas that list potassium bromide as one of the constituent agents, as it has its place in photo chemistry, however, you will not see its use in most of the formulas I put forth in this book. It isn't personal. The formulas I will be highlighting do not use Hydroquinone, which means no superadditivity, which tends to equate with less vigorous oxidation, which is constrained by the sodium sulfite preservative. Well, that's the simple explanation.

SECTION II
Formulas

Understanding photographic formulas is not difficult if attention is paid to the relationships of the constituent elements in the formula. Although that exercise is only useful when one compares what they are seeing in that formula against the outcome after developing the texture text negatives, which you are hopefully holding in your hand. Seeing the formula on paper, and in the negative densities burnishes the connection between the two.

As brought up earlier, a very good comparison can be made between photo chemistry and baking. Both use chemical constituents in various mixtures to arrive at predictable results as pre-visualized before beginning the process. In both cases there is a fuller set of constituent ingredients, out of which various ones can be used to make different outcomes.

When the baker wants light and fluffy pancakes, you know baking powder will be used, and very likely baking soda as well, plus an egg, perhaps two for a richer texture. You would certainly expect a tablespoon of sugar would sweeten the pancakes, as would a dash of vanilla. There is no one recipe for pancakes. They would number as many as there were practicing bakers. It's personal. Those ingredients would be in most of those recipes, and certainly in my pancake recipe.

The above also describes the photographer using the basic principles of black and white photography, and the chemistry that controls the image. Once you have controlled your image, from correct metering and developing, through correctly matching the tonal range to a chosen paper's print range, you will never again allow anyone other than yourself from processing your work. You will have come to understand the artistry of the process, the unique characteristic of each and every photographer. Someone else's process of your image, makes it *their* image.

For the digital black and white photographers out there; good work. Black and white remains pertinent as an art form. Digital manufactures have taken notice and accommodated photographers in general, and off-handedly black and white shooters as well. Epson's printers are an example. Catering to black and white printers, there are now high-resolution printers with three black & white dedicated print heads, for better tonal separation.

Although this book is written for black and white photographers in the dark room, our digital brethren practice the same principles as the chemical cousins. The digital shooters just use Photoshop or Corel's menu item <curves> to replicate the practice of the texture/print test to determine the correct placement of black, then the development for white. Click on and move the line either way to achieve results. Moving that contrast index line in the editing software is equivalent to increased developing time, or change in the dilution of a formula to achieve the same thing.

The results of the print in hand, is the culmination of your actions beforehand. Beginning with choosing the setting (correct metering & placement of value) before clicking the shutter. You know what you had in mind when you set up the scene, then watched the lighting, until *your* scene is set by the value of the lighting. Painting with light. Click.

The photo chemistry that is described in this book is the other half of the process. The wet process after the mechanically inclined latent image process that precedes it. Once the latent image is fixed, only chemical reduction may alter it in any way. The outcome of any latent image is shaped directly by the reduction process. That means by altering your choice of developers (reducing agents) as well as the preserver and accelerator, you effectively alter the outcome of that latent image.

It is this alterable, and shapeable relationship that I use the term artistic expression. It is not a fixed thing. It is what you make of it. The choices you make along the way shapes the vey outcome of your image, through each step of the process. You have the choice to use the averaged light of a wide angle shot of a scene, and that would likely be zone 5 (zone 6, depending), then just shoot, no questions asked, or, you can zero in on one exclusive area of the same scene, then take a reflective meter reading inside a shadowed area, (zone 3 for textural detail) stop down two stops and click. Now it's time for formulas.

Basic formulas:

I shoot in the southwest, where the red spectrum rules. For those photographers who believe it is *more contrasty* down here, do know that there is generally a five-stop range during the day like anywhere else. Panchromatic film is just extra sensitive to that part of the spectrum. If you're looking for a developer that works well for holding in highlights, or very bright elements of the scene, retaining all the highlight texture right to zone 8, then I've got the developer for you.

Beutler 105

I have personally tried out a dozen or so developing formulas, mostly non-commercial, with a wide range of outcomes. What I noticed is that modern films no longer need the super-additivity that film once did. Metol is not known as a high energy developer, but when adding sodium carbonate accelerator, it has the ability to be diluted in various strengths for the various outcomes desired.

H2O @115°	750 ml (cc)	
Metol	5 grams	½ Tbl
Sodium sulfite (anhydrous)	25 grams	1 Tbl + ¼ +1/8 Tsp
Sodium Carbonate (anhydrous)	25 grams	1 Tbl +1 1/8 Tsp
Cold H2O to make	1000 ml	Qt.

~ Standard dilution; 1:10
~ Developing time; Pan-X ISO 50 ~ 7 minutes
FP-4 ISO 125 ~ 8 minutes standard
Tri-X ISO 320/400 ~ 10 minutes possibly

˜ Tank; roll film: continuous agitation for first minute,
15-secs agitation each minute thereafter.
˜ Tray; sheet film: continuous agitation throughout development.

[Expansion by concentration & time]
˜ Dilution 1:7 (expansion N+1) FP-4 ˜ 8 minutes
˜ Dilution 1:5 (expansion N+2) FP-4 ˜ 8 minutes
˜ Dilution 1:10 (expansion N+1) FP-4 ˜ 9 minutes
˜ Dilution 1:10 (expansion N+2) FP-4 ˜ 10 minutes

From the listed dilution & time factors above, it can be seen that a stronger, less diluted developing solution increases the contrast range in a similar way to adding time to the developing process, both extending the tonal range by continuing to increase densities in the upper tonal ranges, including zone 6, 7, and 8. The expansion rates are theoretical; they worked for me at those rates. Those times and dilutions should be tested (texture test).

There is a slight difference between the two. Both increase densities, proportionate to the tonal zone's place in the CI curve. The upper densities nearer the shoulder will proportionally gain density increases from an expansion or extended development time. Their difference is in the softening of highlight densities from the more diluted form, thereby retaining more detail in zone 7. This could likely be bias on my part. I preferred the increased densities for detail, using the compensating effect of Beutler to keep the densities to printable range, matching the chloride paper it would be printed on. Long scale and slower than bromide papers.

When using thick film, such as the old Kodak 250X sheet film, it may need extra time of development, thus possibly adding up to one minute to sheet tray development time. Texture test will show separation of values once they are seen in the resultant test print.

The developing times are beginning points. They would be the developing times to use for the texture text, for identifying zone placement value, and developing time from that point. 8 minutes is a take-off point. A texture test should be the first thing done, to establish a more accurate developing time. As it turns out, 8 minutes was my optimal developing time.

At that time, I was pushing my densities up onto the shoulder and using a softer developing routine to maximize texture and detail in the image. That combination worked well, printed on grade 3 fiber-based print paper, preferably a chloride paper for warm tones. That meant using Kodak's Ektalure G paper. That paper is no longer available, unless you know someone who knows someone.

This formula has no Hydroquinone. It relies on the added sulfite for pH increase as well as sodium carbonate to keep the reduction process working well. This formula is generally used in dilution of 1:10 with water. Not tap water. Boiled or store bought to keep out extra metals and 'stuff' from affecting the developing.

When this formula is kept in a dark bottle in dark dry spaces it will keep for over a month, sometimes many. It is easy to use exactly because it is used in diluted form. Mixing ten parts water with one part of Beutler developer is quick and painless. This formula can also be used in higher concentrations, such as 1:5 or even 1:3. I have tried these dilutions on negatives and can comment. At 1:2 or even theoretically 1:1 for short bursts of development on otherwise well underexposed negatives could make some sense. Even without hydroquinone this formula has developing power in low dilutions.

Of all the developers I have used, this one is my all-time favorite for several reasons. It is cheap and easy to mix and it lasts a long time, and best of all it is a semi-compensating developer. Used in different dilutions increases exponentially its ability to control contrast. By using Beutler in different dilutions will give predictable outcomes to the film's contrast range.

The same three contrast index curves in this diagram show the results of one developer, diluted to three strengths. The stronger the developing mixture the more energetic the reduction, with the result of a higher contrast negative. Another way of saying, an increased contrast index curve.

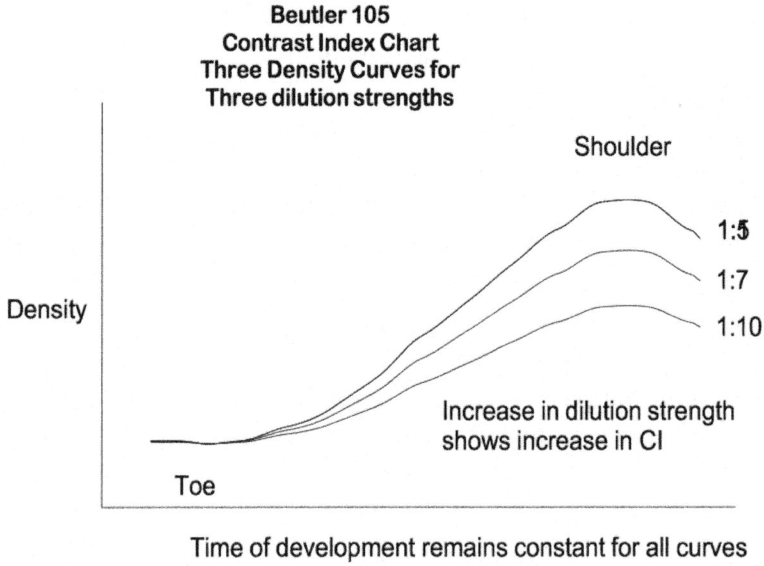

Increasing the strength of the developer by diluting it less is a very handy way of increasing the contrast index of the image, while keeping the developing time constant. This technique can be employed when the setting is very flat and an increase in the tonal range is desired. Using the developer in the more undiluted form increases the development of the higher tonal ranges; 6, 7, 8, as by the time they are developing in the lower tonal values are as dense as they will get, and no further development time can alter that.

This single reducer formula is considered a semi-compensating developer. The term compensating tends to be misunderstood. MQ and other high energy developers aggressively develop the density ranges at the upper end proportionately more than the lower density range, and those are the density ranges that are capable of being pushed to even higher density ranges with continued development, over time.

As mentioned above, Beutler isn't an MQ developer, and is used in a diluted form. Part of the compensation calculous is that the Beutler's compensation is in the form of gently developing the upper range of densities, which keeps intact the texture and detail of those upper ranges, including zone 7, and to a marginal degree zone 8, as without this action those zones tend to be pushed much higher during aggressive developing, losing highlight detail.

Beutler 105 is also known as a tanning developer. The shift in negative color to a chocolate color is indicative of this. The densities will appear thinner than what one might consider a 'normal' negative, as they are more easily seen through. For printing purposes, they are no less dense than standard negatives.

The compensating effect of this formula is evident on densities including zone 6, 7, and 8 respectively. The texture text is to identify exactly where these zones fall, and how much texture is within each textural zone, and, where blank white begins. More than one texture is encouraged for use in comparisons between developers, and developing times. The texture tests show you what you would not otherwise see.

Less of the compensating effect is seen in the lower densities, other than a slight color shift to chocolate. I have successfully produced a negative of an image of my daughter, who has light blonde hair, sitting in full sunlight, which includes full texture and detail in the image, even into the only zone 8 in the shot. I have also used this formula in the 1:7 and 1:5 dilutions to successfully increase the contrast index of very flat scenes, lacking any visible shadow or highlight. Those two dilutions create a very energetic developer.

Expansions & Compactions:

I have shown one method of modifying a formula in order to alter the contrast index, or contrast range of a negative's densities. Although this method is workable, a more precise means of altering the length, and densities of the negative's tonal range, can be accomplished using an expansion method. Or, if one wants to keep the densities down, by shortening the tonal range that would otherwise be too long, compaction is the method.

As has been mentioned before, during the reduction process of development the chosen formula and the time of development proportionately affect the tonal ranges *above* zone 5. The lower tonal ranges develop to their full potential by the time zone 5 has been developed, and no amount of developing time after that will change their densities, respectively. The tonal ranges (zones) that will be affected begin with zone 6 and become increasingly so moving up through zone 8, which is affected the most.

Thus, a compensating developer works most effectively when those upper tonal ranges need to be held in check. Even when a compensating developer is used, there are times when the light creates more measurable stops of light between the two texture zones, and further retardation of development in the upper range is desirable. That method is compaction. That method is simply deducting developing time. A good beginning is 1 minute less development to equal a 1 stop decrease in the tonal range. Also referred to a N – 1. To decrease the tonal range by two, equals an N – 2 compaction, or two minutes less developing time. These are beginning points to use when doing the texture test.

Conversely, an expansion is the opposite, adding one or two minutes to the development time to increase the density range by one, or two density ranges respectively. These methods are used in conjunction with metering, determining how many full stops are represented by the tonal ranges of the scene.

The count centers around the two textural zones; zone 3 & zone 7. If there is a natural four stop difference between these two zones, then it can be said that there is a natural five-stop day, in lighting terms. It should be understood that if one is measuring an identifiable zone 7 in a scene, then there should be an identifiable zone 8 as well, indicating that normal development will give the full eight stop range for paper printing.

Understanding expansion or compaction has to do with shaping and defining the expected densities of your negative in the top three density ranges on any given negative. Zone 6, 7, & 8. Those three zones are effectively the only three zones that you are able to alter, either through dilution of the developing agent or time of chemical development. Those three zones, however have everything to do with how much texture and detail you want in your photograph. Where you wish to place your first tonal density; zone 1, is of equal importance, and will of course affect all the tonal ranges above.

I cannot stress enough the importance the simple textured towel text is for setting up your development procedure. That very procedure will define your negative, your final image. The possibility of having full control over the densities of your negative has to do with understanding the relationships between placement of tonal value (metering) and developing regimen (formula/time).

Seeing the actual textural print evidence before you will tell you exactly which one of those black film densities is the one wanted, in order to show full shadow detail. From that density, move down two stops (zone 3 to zone 1) and that is the density that will begin the lower scale of your negative, nearest the toe. Nothing more will change things after you click the shutter.

From the textural density that you chose to represent full shadow detail (zone 3) count up four densities, to arrive at zone 7, the second textural zone/density. That should be four stops, which would mean five stops to zone 8 (blank white). Whatever difference you get from measuring zone 3 from zone 8, you compensate by using the principles of expansion/compaction; either change dilution strength of the developer, or, add/subtract developing time. That can only alter the tonal ranges above zone 5.

Fine Grain Developer: D-23

H_2O @ 115°F	750 ml (cc)	
Metol	7.5 grams	2 1/8 Tsp
Sodium Sulfite (Anhydrous)	100 grams	4 Tbl + 1 Tsp
Cold Water to make	1000 ml (cc)	

Use; Undiluted {I used it at 1:2}

~ Developing time;	Pan-X ISO 50	~ 6 ½ minutes
	FP-4 ISO 125	~ 8 minutes standard
	Tri-X ISO 320/400	~ 9 minutes possibly

~ Tank; roll film: continuous agitation for first minute,
15-secs agitation each minute thereafter.
~ Tray; sheet film: continuous agitation throughout development

As fine grain developers go, I have found D-23 to be exemplary. It can also be very a versatile developer, with the ability to be used in dilutions for desired compensating effects, but is normally used undiluted. Notice the absence of any alkaline carbonate agents. The preservative agent, sodium sulfite, in this formula is quadrupled from the Beutler formula, and in that quantity, it begins acting not only as an accelerator, but moving into the arena of being considered a reducing agent.

Being used in full concentrate form, it is of course easy for use, and it's shelf life is good when in air tight dark bottles in low light storage. D-23 can be used in diluted form. I have not made a science of that dilution rate/time as I never needed to. What I can say about it from experience is that if serious compensation is needed and time isn't an issue, then this formula can be diluted down to work over long developing periods and remain active.

As noted in the formula, to use undiluted, that is the original formulas' use. I have developed negatives using D-23 undiluted. It works well. However, as also noted earlier, I was pushing my contrast index range up into the shoulder region, by resetting my ISO rating lower, theoretically 'overexposing' the shot. I wanted to melt down all the available silver halide in the emulsion that was possible. I used ISO 80 for ISO 125 rated films. Therefore, I wanted a bit softer developing agent that would offer a compensating effect on the upper densities that might otherwise get out of hand with a more energetic developer. For that I used D-23 usually diluted to 1:2. A good example of dilution follows.

I had the opportunity to photograph the bronze statues of an artist that had retired from Disney, working on Fantasia. I had but one opportunity to make this happen so I wanted to be ready. I used a Century Graflex 6x9 camera in soft natural north light setup against black background. I metered (I thought) and shot away, with constant light, theoretically not needing to re-meter. . .

When it was done and I had taken leave, sitting in my dark room on the stool at the mixing table, looking over the shoot's notes in the book. It is there that I came to realize that my conversion during the light metering stage was two stops off. Confessions as they are, invectives and possibly rough language was heard for some distance upon fuller realization. There was no re-dos.

So, time to test out the real capabilities of these compensating developers. I diluted D-23 to 1:10, then developed the alternative negative I most wanted for just over 20-minutes. I was feeling confident. As the developing Gods will from time to time, I was tapped to succeed. I had chosen the correct reducing process for this particular need. I unveiled the negative in light, after fixing of course, to find an image that was an amazingly detailed, full range negative, that looked 3-D.

Without Hydroquinone, and super-additivity, without carbonates as an accelerant, Metol and sodium sulfite in unison carried out the task, which called for soft, low energy reduction, with sufficient alkaline from the sodium sulfite, to keeping the reducing process active over a long developing time. At the same time the sulfite kept fog at bay. The sodium sulfite was acting as both *preservative* and *restrainer*.

Black and white photography can be explained and applied in near mathematical formulations with laboratory controlled, precise measuring and strict timing, but it doesn't have to be. The precise measuring and strict timing thing though, it is pretty important for consistency. The photographer has to think of black and white photography as a malleable process. A process that can be adapted and applied photographically to represent the pre-visualized image in a fine art print.

The formulas I am highlighting in this book are old formulas, known for over a century. Both are easily available. You just have to mix them. So far, you only need three constituent chemicals. From a cursory browse of cyber shopping indicates the prices for photo chemicals have risen over the past thirty years. It would have been roughly half the cost back then, but it must be kept in mind these are bulk chemicals and they will make enough developer to process for a year. Unless you're Paul Strand or Ed Vliek. Then you might get six months' worth.

The thesis of this book is this simple thought. As a photographer, you have tools to apply when making the photographic image. The beginning of that process commences when the photographer clicks the shutter release. The latent image is now formed. The aperture/speed ratio setting applied, sets up the original tonal range potential. Development then fosters the preconceived outcome.

The formulas I have offered as a starting point, have both demonstrated their strengths, in the first case I needed to hold back highlight development to retain texture and detail, while keeping full detail in the shadow area as well. That constitutes a compaction. Shortening the density range on the negative, from what might be a thirteen-stop shot, down to eight stops. Shoot for zone 3 so the details remain in the shadow and develop for the highlights, keeping the upper densities in a textural range as well.

The second case required a slow acting, yet long working formula that wouldn't over-develop the upper densities of an otherwise well over-exposed negative. That soft developer was D-23 in diluted form. It can never be known, yet in theory, the Beutler formula's carbonate accelerator would likely have over-developed the negative in its overexposed state.

There is yet another formula that for adventurous photographers would benefit your work; Pyrocatechin, mainly for acutance and tonal length, both of which are available with this developer. That's next.

Pyrocatechin (Pyro)
Windish Pyro;

Part A:

H2o @ 115°F	750 ml (cc)
Sodium Sulfite	80.0 grams
Pyrocatechin	12.5 grams
Cold Water to make	1000 ml

Part B:

Sodium Hydroxide	10% solution
Dilution;	25 ml solution A
	15 ml solution B
	960 ml H2o

FP-4	ISO 125	~ 10 minutes standard
Tri-X	ISO 320/400	~ 13 minutes possibly

~ Tank; roll film: continuous agitation for first minute,
15-secs agitation each minute thereafter.
~ Tray; sheet film: continuous agitation throughout development

This formula does not have a good shelf life. Pyrocatechin is very sensitive to air and oxidizes rapidly. When fresh, Pyrocatechin is a white flake, repeated opening of the chemical jar over a period of a week or so shows the flakes beginning to turn a tan color, and eventually a chocolate brown, with the chemical potency reducing over that time span, and discoloration.

I modified the original formula to allow me to mix only the portion of developer I needed at the time. A throw away formula.

Solution:

To 1 oz H2o	@ 110° Add	3 ml (10% solution) sodium sulfite
	then stir in	¼ Tsp Pyrocatechin
	[Optional]	1/8 Tsp Metol (for super-additivity)

Tank Development;	[24oz]	15 ml solution
	Add	735 ml H2o
	Add	4.5 ml (10% sol) sodium hydroxide
	[16oz]	10 ml solution
	Add	490 ml H2o
	Add	3 ml (10% sol) sodium hydroxide

This formula is very energetic due to the sodium hydroxide accelerator. Beginning development time is slightly longer than the Beutler formula, which might seem a bit strange being this formula uses the hydroxide compared to Beutler's sodium carbonate accelerator, however, the compensating element of this formula keeps the upper densities intact even during longer developing times. The developing times shown above are starting points, which one would use for texture test development.

Developing time remains the same as it is the same formula re-jiggered to be used once then thrown away. I have used this formula in a tray with sheet film, but I used it more for roll film development to enhance acutance and high definition, which this formula does quite well. Very long tonal scale with excellent mid toned grays, rich blacks and crisp whites.

Each developer has its own characteristic abilities. Choose your developer for the task you have at hand. All three of these developers can be considered fine grain developers. Pyrocatechin is also a full compensating developer, meaning it has a tanning action that works over the entire tonal range. This enhances shadow detail on the lower end as well as holds in detail at the upper end of the tonal range.

There are other Pyrocatechin formulas available. One primary difference in them is the accelerator. The Windish Pyro formula uses sodium hydroxide, which is one of the most volatile agents in the arsenal. I suggest using that chemical in a pre-mixed 10% solution due to its volatility. Mixing in even a couple grams of the dry chemical in a flask of even cold water can make the water boil and splash solution. Just be aware.

Pyrocatechin ˜ 2 Solution
(with Sodium Carbonate)

Solution A:

H2O @ 115°F	350 ml	
Sodium Sulfite (Anhydrous)	20 grams	½ Tbl + 1 1/8 Tsp
Pyrocatechin	10 grams	2 ½ Tsp
cold water to make	500 ml	

Solution B:

H2O @ 115°F	350 ml	
Potassium Carbonate	60 grams	3 Tbl + 1 Tsp
cold water to make	500 ml	

Dilution: Equal Parts A: B
Developing Time; 7 minutes

Potassium Metabisulfite is best used instead of sodium sulfite for longer storage of the solution. The reason for separate solutions in the first place is keeping the accelerator separate from the pyro reducer, for better shelf life. How much shelf life depends on how fast the mixed solution is being used.

A good many developing formulas use sodium carbonate as the accelerator. In this case potassium carbonate was used, and for that I have no answer, as I have used a pyro formula using the sodium-based form. If these two accelerators are changed in the formula be sure to look at the equivalents chart in the last section to see the conversion. 100 parts sodium carbonate, equals 167 parts potassium carbonate. If you already use sodium carbonate with other formulas then it is easy to alter the above formula by converting the weight difference.

I am including two more Pyrocatechin formulas to show the versatility and range of this developing agent. You will see in the formulas how altering the constituents changes the developing action, which directly affects the tonal range, characteristic of the CI curve, as well as definition and detail. The first is a one solution tanning formula.

Pyrocatechin ~ Tanning:

H2o @ 115°F	750 ml
Sodium Sulfite (Anhydrous)	5 grams
Pyrocatechin	2 grams
Sodium Hydroxide	10 ml (10 % sol)
cold water to make	1000 ml

dilution: Use undiluted

FP-4	ISO 125	~ 15 minutes standard
Tri-X	ISO 320/400	~ 20 minutes possibly

~ Tank; roll film: continuous agitation for first minute, 15-secs agitation each minute thereafter.

~ Tray; sheet film: continuous agitation throughout development

Notice in this Pyro formula the chemical ratios, as well as the relatively smaller amounts of preservative and reducers, yet with a relatively higher yield of accelerator. This developer is used undiluted, then thrown away, thus making it far more likely that a liter bottle of can be used up before spoiling.

The small amount of preservative, in the form of sodium sulfite, is not enough to hold back the natural tanning action of the Pyro, thereby increasing the tanning ability. Chocolate brown negatives, with full compensating effects, both low tonal values as well as high tonal values. The compensating affect is more pronounced in the upper densities, simply because those top three density ranges continue to be affected by development over time, unlike the first five density ranges, which all reach their density maximum and remain there, no matter how much further the developing continues.

Compensating developers work best in keeping the upper densities in check on bright sunlit days with reflective textures that meter at or above zone 7. Meter for textural zone 3, then find the brightest reflective object in the scene and meter again and if those two readings exceed five stops, compaction is in order, or the above formula might be employed.

For those photographers that photograph in the southwest U.S., the spectral quality of light is shifted to the red end of the spectrum, and for panchromatic film that tends to make the image more "contrasty". The truth is panchromatic film is much more sensitive to red than blue. The real affect being that this red shifted light pings the negative with what the meter is reading, as in any other shot, yet affects the sensitized silver halide in the emulsion more than when the spectral light is more to the blue side.

It is helpful to understand how a particular formula works by observing the constituent elements. You have seen formulas with three of the basic constituent elements. The Reducer, Preservative and Accelerator, using five chemicals; Metol & Pyrocatechin [reducers], sodium sulfite, [preservative] sodium carbonate, potassium carbonate, sodium hydroxide, [accelerators].

The next Pyro formula includes a Restrainer for the first time. The restrainer is used when the preservative is insufficient alone to keep reducing agent from oxidizing, thereby creating 'fog'. The single reducer formulas shown in this book normally do not need the restrainer, as their makeup doesn't create the conditions for a need to restrain the reducing process during development.

One of the best ways to understand the differences between the formulas listed in this book is by comparing the chemical elements of the formulas, by their weight respectively, as well as their respective combinations in each formula. When making comparisons, keep in mind their constituent task, and you begin to see how they interrelate, and when combined, how they affect the densities of the negative.

Pyrocatechin ~ Non-Staining

H2o @ 115°F	300 ml
sodium Sulfite (Anhydrous)	50 grams
Pyrocatechin	20 grams
sodium hydroxide	16 grams
Potassium Bromide (restrainer)	2 grams
cold water to make	400 ml

Dilution:	1:10 ~ 1:15	
FP-4	ISO 125	~ 5 minutes standard
Tri-X	ISO 320/400	~ 8-10 minutes possibly

~ Tank; roll film: continuous agitation for first minute, 15-secs agitation each minute thereafter.

~ Tray; sheet film: continuous agitation throughout development

This formula is much more concentrated, which explains the dilution ratios. The higher dilution ratio will show more compensating effect on the negative, for a softer CI curve. The total amount of developing solution is less than half the normal liter mixture, an amount that can be used up while it is still fresh.

It goes without saying. . . that the dilution amount as well as developing time are beginning points from which to do a texture text, to see exactly where your densities lie on the tonal scale, which tells you where to place your shot, and length of developing time, respective to each developing formula.

I have said in the early part of this book that I would not be listing or talking about MQ developers. In that vein I remain in the preferred camp of non-MQ developers. However, in the larger conversation on developing I believe it is also a good idea to take a moment to discuss probably the most currently used developer at this time. D-76, a negative developer, and Dektol, Kodak is a print developer, respectively.

D-76 is a good developer. It is an MQ developer, using both Metol and Hydroquinone in the formula, constituting the super-additivity relationship. It is a semi-high energy developer that is clean, fast acting and has a long shelf life. I would almost bet there is more of that solution used in developing than any other, ever. However, I believe there are better formulas for use in today's films. Especially for high definition and highlight densities with texture and detail. The formula;

D-76:

H2O @ 115°F	750 ml
Metol	2 grams
Sodium Sulfite (Anhydrous)	100 grams
Hydroquinone	5 grams
Kodalk	2 grams
cold water to make	1000 ml

Dilution:

General use 1:1

Film Type A ~ 25-50 ISO	7 minutes
Film Type B ~ 100-125 ISO	9 minutes
Film Type C ~ 320-400 ISO	11 minutes

It is easy to now notice the added ingredients to the formula; Hydroquinone and Kodalk. The Hydroquinone is the second reducer, and a high energy one. This increased energy is primarily from the super-additivity. What appears in the formula as no accelerator is a bit misleading. Kodalk includes a small amount of sodium hydroxide. 100g sodium metaborate (Kodalk) = 45.45g borax + 9.53g NaOH (sodium hydroxide).

The published formula for D-76 recommends using 29.0 grams of borax as an accelerator. However, in its packaged developer, Kodak uses balanced alkali (Kodalk). It is easy enough to substitute balanced alkali for the same weight of borax. Development time should be decreased by approximately 15% to compensate for the higher pH.

Another combination of this formula is D-76H, which omits hydroquinone in the formula and increases the amount of Metol_to 2.5 grams. D-76H can be used in the same way as D-76, including development times. This formula then, now becomes something very much like D-23, with a diluted accelerator; balanced alkali & sodium hydroxide. Both formulas then all but match, as well as become a fine grain, compensating developers.

Carbonates or sodium hydroxide used as accelerators in the earlier formulas replace the working action of the two developer combination of this formula. The difference in developing action is that in using the carbonate instead of a second reducer is that it becomes a finer grain developer, as well as a more compensating developer.

There are dozens more formulas to draw from, many of which are variations upon the theme. I have shown six formulas, four of which are Pyrocatechin developers, each of which are formulated to do specific tasks. Another reason for these formulas is they all can be formulated from a short list of bulk chemicals to have on hand. That includes two reducers, the developing agents, the preservative, sodium sulfite, potentially three accelerators, Sodium Carbonate-Potassium Carbonate and Sodium Hydroxide, of which only one need be used at a time, and a restrainer, Potassium Bromide.

Over the years I had two dozen bottles and jars of chemicals, with the ability to mix pretty much any formula I had ever come across, which includes a lot of formulas. I also realized over those many years that I only needed three or four of those formulas to cover every developing need. The formulas in this book are capable of handling any shooting situation, giving stunning negatives. Stunning for me is looking through a negative to see distinctly separated tonalities with high acutance and good textural detail and overall brightness.

The controls needed to attain beautiful negatives is in the selected developer formula, fined tuned to fit the metered shot. The photographer needs to know: how many stops does the meter read between the shadow area (zone 3) and the brightest object or surface in the shot (zone 8). If that difference is five photographic stops, then you have an eight-stop tonal spread, and normal development will keep those tonal densities intact on the negative.

In earlier iterations of talking about tonal zones, focusing on the two textural zones that merit metering; zone 3 (shadow detail) and zone 7 (whites with full detail). That is because those two zones control the upper and lower range of tonal possibilities by their placement, then development respectively. Zone 8 is considered as well as that tonal density reaches the end of printing possibilities at paper base white. Knowing that point is important.

Should the metered scene show a six-stop difference between zone 3 and zone 8, then normal development would push the upper densities too far, and an N-1 compaction would be needed. That is 1 minute less in development as a beginning point. Again, that is exactly what the texture text is for. Negatives right in front of your eyes that have the actual tonal range, with visible texture in some. Plotting your chosen point of reference is the part the exercise is all about.

After developing your texture test negatives it is advised to print a test strip, on the paper you intend to print on. You will then have a test strip of ten negative densities. Find that tonal range (density) in the lower end that just begins to show full textural detail. What YOU want that zone to look like, how much texture. That becomes zone 3. Count up five density ranges towards the whites. The last and final density range in a print is pure white, paper base white. This zone has no detail or texture, nothing. Pure white.

If the number of densities from the shadow detail in zone 3, to pure white of zone 8, is five stops, then the developing time for that developer is right on. That metering placement, then developer/time becomes; *normal.* If the count is six stops, develop one minute less, if the count is four stops, then N+1, and expansion, is needed. This is how you tune the placement and development of the negative to arrive at that handshake that gives your negatives a tonal range that fits well with the printable tonal range of the selected print paper.

It is on the paper that your negative will become the photograph. If your negative doesn't fit well with the paper you will print on, then you do not have the image you want. It will either be flat, gray or have lost the middle-tone and highlight detail, leaving only uninspiring print on the paper. Think Edward Weston, with his print clarity and match to the bromide paper he printed on. That's the possibility.

SECTION 3
Stop Baths & Fixers

Completing the Process:

I have only touched upon the subject of black and white photo chemistry possibilities. There are also many chemical formulas and developers I have not discussed or even mentioned. The intent of this book is not a full education of black and white photography. That would demand several volumes of unfathomable amounts of necessary material. The intent of this book is to familiarize the reader with basic photographic principles that, when applied, give the reader, as photographer, full control over their negatives, and reciprocally, their finished print.

Experience has demonstrated that in modern films there is no longer any need for an MQ developer. It is my personal belief that the only reason for this is that it is the only standard commercial pre-packaged formula available. Mixing your own developing formulas in today's world is amazingly easy, and cheap, with digital gram scales, plastic containers for mixing and the internet for ordering bulk chemicals.

Completing the developing process includes stopping the reduction of the latent image, then removing all the remaining silver halide from the emulsion, which clears all the remaining density area surrounding the latent image, where no light has reached the emulsion. This process is the *fixing* stage of development. This is what makes the negative stable and permanent over time. The first step is stopping the reduction process.

Stop Baths:

After a negative, or print has gone through development, the first step is stopping the developing action. The simplest way to do this is place the developed negative, or print, in running water, to dilute and rinse out the developing agent. This is not the preferred method of ceasing the development. The preferred method would be to use a *stop bath.* The stop bath is a weak acidic solution that immediately arrests the reduction process, an alkaline solution.

Stop baths are varied, and can be mixed using a variety of chemicals that are acid based. In many instances a weak acidic solution of 2% glacial acetic acid, or a 3-5% solution of potassium metabisulphite or sodium metabisulphite. These agents alone only go towards arresting the developing process quickly, by their acidic nature working against the alkaline developer.

The negative or print will have swelled somewhat during the developing stage so it is sometimes advisable to add a hardening agent to the stop bath. This can be done simply enough by adding Potassium (Chrome) Alum to the acetic acid. The Potassium Alum can also be used alone in an increased amount. The point of the stop bath is to stop all development of the negative or print while forming the basis of an acid environment.

Below are four variations of a stop bath. The acidic agents are still available in various outlets, including online ordering. They are easy to mix and have good shelf life, so they are easy to keep on hand. As noted above, each of those stop baths are also considered to be emulsion hardening. This helps protect the negative emulsion from damage during processing.

Stop Bath & Hardening Formulas

Chemicals	SB1 AN216	SB3	170	172 D25
Acetic Glacial Acid	17 grams			6.5 ml 10% sol
Potassium Alum (Chrome Alum)		30 grams		15 grams
Potassium Metabisulphite			50 grams	
Water To Make	1000 cc	1000 cc	1000 cc	1000 cc

There are more variations of stop baths and chemical agents to make that happen. However, I see no real need to create a full listing of every agent or mixture simply because the above four do the job well and are easily located and purchased. The key here is the KISS method.

As always, there are other methods to use as a stop bath. Vinegar is one of them. White vinegar comes in 5% concentration, which can be mixed with distilled water to 1% solution to make a workable stop bath. For negatives, a water wash is sufficient for most uses, filling the developing tank two or three times with fresh rinse water before adding fixer is generally adequate.

For prints, however, the emulsion is much thicker, with the paper also absorbing more of the developing agent, making further rinsing important. A one-minute immersion in the rinsing tray, with flowing water should be sufficient to rinse the vast majority of developing agent out of the paper emulsion. Thirty seconds in a mild acidic bath is the most certain way of stopping the developing process completely.

Fixing Baths:

So much can be said of fixing baths, or fixers, and I will attempt to address the issues involved. There are many. The basic character of the fixing bath should be acidic, which is counter to the alkaline pH of the developer you want to neutralize in order to arrest development. Once the negative emulsion, or paper has been saturated with the developing solution, it takes time or chemical action to stop the process.

Early in photographic history the term *Hypo* was synonymous with the fixing process with that process utilizing Sodium Hyposulphite as the fixing agent, hence Hypo. As will any fixing agent, sodium Hyposulphite infuses itself with the emulsion and needs to be washed out. The amount of available silver in the negative or print emulsion is far more than is used up by the reduced silver in the latent image.

All those unused silver salts, now interacting with the sodium Hyposulphite which forms a double-salt. Once all the milky silver bromide has been removed by the sodium Hyposulphite, leaving clear film, or clear print, the fixing is not yet complete. That double salt built up of Hyposulphite crystals and silver salts remains in the emulsion and needs continued washing for as many minutes that it took to clear the negative, or print. Left on the emulsion to dry, that double salt becomes insoluble. No amount of washing can change that. Your negative or print will deteriorate over time.

Even in the very early years of photography it was understood that Ammonia was an alternative to sodium Hyposulphite. So was Potassium Cyanide, although there is clear reason to be wary of using that as a fixing agent in the standard darkroom. The problem with Ammonia was at that time, for *fast fixing* Ammonia needed to be in strong solution, which softened the emulsion and did damage therein.

My experience with mixing fixing agents is primarily with acid hardening fixing solutions. When it comes to self-mixing stop baths and fixers I leave that up to the individual's own preferences and procedures. Developing formulas shape the very image in question. They matter in a direct way. Stop baths and fixers need only satisfy their respective task of stopping development, then removing all leftover traces of silver halide salts. Whether they are commercially purchased or simply mixed in the darkroom is immaterial. My personal procedure was to mix anything I needed, as I had the space, and money, to keep the chemical shelf stocked.

As mentioned above, elements needed for those activities can be found at the local grocery store, and work as well as any commercial product to get the job done. Just understand what you are using and how to make it work properly. The results are the same if done right.

Fixing Solutions:

There are two types of fixing solutions. Hardening and non-hardening. Although this is almost self-evident, the simple explanation being that during development, the emulsion will swell, on both the negative and print. The emulsion on the negative is thin, on a non-soluble substratum. The emulsion on the print is much thicker, on a soluble backing. Only the upper densities representing the highlights come near the full depth of the emulsion.

Not using an acid hardening fixer, this swelling remains until the emulsion is entirely dry, with shrinkage being a small issue, if it even affects the outcome. Scratching or damage to the emulsion surface being the first issue. Thus, the advent of hardening fixers. One heuristic value of these hardening fixers is that they work in higher temperatures.

I will list both, not only to allow those that do not want to harden the emulsion, for whatever reason, to do so, as well as for the ability of the reader to view the differences between the formulas to see how each constituent agent works.

Non-Hardening fixing Baths:

#158 Rapid Fix

H20 @ 125°F	750 ml
Ammonium Thiosulfate (Crystals)	150 grams
Sodium (or) Potassium Metabisulfite	20 grams
cold water to make	1000 ml

Clearing Time:

Negatives ~ 1 1/2-2 minutes ~ Full fixing time; 4 minutes
Prints ~ 1 minute ~ Full fixing time; 5 minutes

#159 Acid Fix

H2o @ 125°F	750 ml
Sodium Thiosulfate (Crystals)	250 grams
Sodium Sulfite (Anhydrous)	10 grams
Acetic Acid	15 grams
cold water to make	1000 ml

Clearing Time:
Negatives ~ 2-3 minutes ~ Full fixing time; 6 minutes
Prints ~ 4-5 minutes ~ Full fixing time; 10 minutes

~ Times are based upon best practices as offered in various sources, as well as personal experience.

~ Acetic Acid is best used in liquid form. The standard being a 28% solution. 3 parts chemical to 8 parts water gives you the 28% mixture. Convert the liquid to dry using; 2.8 ml = 1 gram = 42 ml of 28% solution for the 10 grams of in the above formula. (Also see Equivalents, Weights & Measures)

These two fixers represent the basic modern fixer. Notice the added weight of sodium thiosulfate necessary to equal the weight of the ammonia. The ammonium thiosulfate is a faster acting fixer than the sodium thiosulfate, if minutes are important, as a processing matter for the photographer.
(See Equivalents)

Acid Hardening Fixing Baths:

The acid hardening fixing baths do one extra job when washing out all the unused silver halide in the emulsion. The potassium alum, also known as Chrome Alum, hardens the emulsion as the thiosulfate is reducing the silver halide in the emulsion to a non-binding salt form held by the acidic solution. As noted above, that fixing process must proceed past the point where visual inspection indicates that the cloudy bromide emulsion is no longer present, as evidenced by the clarity of the negative.

What won't be seen visually is the residue of double salt brought about by the thiosulfate and the silver halide. That double salt must be removed entirely for the negative, or print, to be of archival quality. I am listing several fixers, using the variations based on the constituent element. There should be a wide range of useful formulas at hand, as each one has its benefit to the process, either because it does a particular task, and/or because it doesn't interfere with some other element of the process. The photographer should have workable solutions for any contingency that arises.

F15/PIF;

H2O @ 125°F	750 ml
Sodium Thiosulfate (Crystals)	240 grams
Sodium Sulfite (Anhydrous)	15 grams
Acetic Glacial Acid (28% solution)	48 ml
Boric Acid	7.5 grams
Potassium Alum (hardener)	15 grams
cold water to make	1000 ml

Clearing Time:

Negatives ~	2-3 minutes ~	Full fixing time; 6 minutes
Prints ~	4-5 minutes ~	Full fixing time; 10 minutes

F6;

H2o @ 125°F	750 ml
Sodium thiosulfate (Crystals)	240 grams
Sodium Sulfite (Anhydrous)	15 grams
Acetic Glacial Acid (28% solution)	48 ml
Kodalk	15 grams
Potassium (Chrome) Alum	15 grams
cold water to make	1000 ml

Clearing Time:
Negatives ~ 2-3 minutes ~ Full fixing time; 6 minutes
Prints ~ 4-5 minutes ~ Full fixing time; 10 minutes

ATF5 ~ Rapid Acid Hardening Bath

H2o @ 125°F	750 ml
Ammonium Thiosulfate (Crystals)	200 grams
Sodium Sulfite (Anhydrous)	15 grams
Acetic Glacial Acid (28% solution)	55 ml
Boric Acid	7.5 grams
Potassium (Chrome) Alum	15 grams
cold water to make	1000 ml

ATF2 ~ Rapid Acid Hardening Bath

H2o @ 125°F	750 ml
Ammonium Thiosulfate (Crystals)	1 12 grams
Sodium Sulfite (Anhydrous)	15 grams
Potassium (Chrome) Alum	15 grams
cold water to make	1000 ml

* See fixing times and dilutions below:

The two above rapid acid hardening fixing baths do reduce fixing time, if that is a concern for the photographer. There are instances when using a Pyrocatechin formula that the ammonium does not mix well during the fixing process, in which case the sodium base thiosulfate is to be used. I had come across that precaution once, but it did alert me to potential pitfalls of using ammonium thiosulfate.

It is less likely that one might run into trouble using ammonium thiosulfate during negative fixing than when printing, as the paper emulsion is much thicker, holding in more of the chemistry during each phase, thereby being more susceptible to chemical interactions that cause problems. The only problem with fixer had to do with Pyrocatechin with the ammonium thiosulfate during printing. It was more of a caution.

The best rule to follow is the visual test for fixing; my words. The amount of time it takes for a fixing solution to remove all the bromide emulsion from the negative, rendering it clear, is halfway point. Add that amount of time for the final fixing, when the double-salt is being reduced and rinsed off. Being prints can be visually observed during their entire process, under a safe light, clearing is a bit less obvious, but can be observed, as those that have been printing for a while know. I personally followed a baseline rule of ten minutes in a fixing bath, with intermittent agitation for anything I wanted to consider archival.

I have listed clearing times for negatives in the above material based upon my processing experiences over the years. If there were to be any doubt on any level of processing, I erred on the side archival caution. I never felt the need to hurry or cut corners. That tends to lead to ugly disasters. The below charts reflect established fixing times fromthe publication as the source, as noted above the charts.

Clearing Times in Sodium Thiosulfate
C. I. Jacobson ~ "Developing" [C. E. K. Mees]

Sodium Thiosulfate %	13 °C 55 °F	18 °C 65 °F	24 °C 75 °F
	Time in Minutes		
10.00%	(Longer Than) 10	9 ½	7
15.00%	8	7 ½	5
20.00%	6	4 ½	4

Clearing Times In Sodium and Ammonium Thiosulfate
C. I. Jacobson ~ "Developing" [C. E. K. Mees]

Concentration	{at 20 °C) Sodium Thiosulfate Time in Minutes	Ammonium Thiosulfate Time in Minutes
10.00%	7	2
20.00%	5	1 ½
30.00%	3 ½	½
$40.00	3 ½	½

As is disclosed above, these clearing times come from the book "Developing" which I have found to be invaluable in understanding black and white photo chemistry and processing principles in general. It is easy to see the relationships between sodium and ammonium thiosulfate, and the range of dilutions each offers. These times can be taken as accurate assuming that the fixing solution hasn't become exhausted from use. Knowing when to refresh your fixer is very important. It can also be very valuable when you take it in to run through a centrifuge to recover your cake silver bars.

When to Change Fixing Bath

C. I. Jacobson ~ "Developing" [C. E. K. Mees]

Size of Film	Number Per Liter
8x10 Sheet Film or Fiber Based Photo Paper	25
4x5 Sheet Film	100
6cm x 9cm Sheet Film	150
120 Roll Film	25
35mm Roll Film (36 Exposures)	25

Hypo Clear:

The Hypo Clear agent is used to rid the negative or print of all vestiges of the fixing agent, mainly the thiosulfate. Water washing can, of itself completely wash the fixer out of the negative or print. Those wash times can become long, being advised at 30 minutes of wash time for a print, then left in a hypo-eliminator for 6 minutes (at 68°-70°), then a final wash of 10 minutes.

Hypo Remover: Negatives

Sodium Carbonate or Bicarbonate 10% solution
Use 5 minutes then wash ten minutes

Hypo Remover: Paper Prints

Water (Distilled)		20 ounces	500 cc
Hydrogen Peroxide	3% solution	5 ounces	125 cc
Ammonia	3% solution	4 ounces	100 cc
Water to make		40 ounces	1000 cc

Hypo Remover: Dilution

H2o @ 125°F	750 ml
Sodium Sulfite	200 grams
Sodium Bisulfite	2 grams
cold water to make	1000ml

Dilute: 1:9 for use
Use 5 minutes then wash ten minutes

It is up to each photographer to know how much of the developing process they wish to control. It is easy to reach over and dig out a few cups of Bisquick when baking, but then, mixing your own Bisquick takes four ingredients and less than two minutes to accomplish. All you need are measuring spoons. Interestingly enough it is the same with photo chemistry. The weight measurements of each chemical you could possibly use is listed in the final part of this book. All you need for measurement is measuring spoons.

Those that have taken the time to make it to this point in the book are serious about their photography. If you know what an expansion or a compaction is in photographic terms you are ahead of the curve for understanding one of the controls in photo chemistry of this craft. It should now be easier to see the photographic process as stages of setting up the final image.

The Print

The photographic image begins when the photographer sees what she wants to capture. That scene, that face or that person sitting at a table outdoors, or an object, in just the right light. That exact image as a relationship of light onto a scene. Painting with light. The light is everything, and knowing your metering and placement of values sets up that relationship so that it can be processed, after it becomes a latent image in the film emulsion.

That process then needs to keep the relationship to those metered tonal values, and has to be predictable, both developer characteristic and time. That metering and placement, then chemical reduction process, must, in the end, match the tonal range of the printing paper to be used. If that final black and white curve, represented by stepped densities of the negative don't match the paper's tonal range, the process is pretty much useless.

What to take away from all this is simply that black and white photography is a malleable process, allowing for a great deal of personalization of expression. There are good rule of thumb beginning points which you can experiment with. As I have said, I preferred to push my densities up toward the shoulder of the curve to gain as much density and detail of each tonal range as possible, while at the same time keeping the total tonal range within eight full stops. This, I could match to my preferred paper at the time, Kodak's Ektalure G.

Placing your densities along the contrast index curve should be done after the texture test, to best decide which density range you prefer, according to the textural zones. As a beginning point, altering the ISO a third stop either up or down will effectively move the tonal range of the negative up or down the contrast index curve respectively.

My preference was to move the density range up the curve towards the shoulder. An example of that is the image on the cover of this book. I set my ISO rating to 80 when shooting FP4 rated at 125, theoretically "overexposing" a bit. I also chose a non MQ compensating developer to hold in the higher density ranges. I also did texture tests to define the correct developing time.

To move the density range lower, you would simply reset the ISO of a 125 rated film to ISO 160, thereby moving the density range lower, towards the toe of the curve. Do texture texts because you will likely need to extend developing time slightly to ensure the higher densities reach their preferred ranges, respectively. Less light on the emulsion necessitates more aggressive development to achieve the same densities in an equivalent emulsion having received more light.

These are examples of how a photographer has the ability to shape their images in very personalized ways. For those shooting with sheet film, each shot can be customized entirely to a desired ending, matched of course to the printing paper to be used. For photographers shooting roll film, expansions and compactions, ISO setting changes and other primary changes to the latent image must be dedicated to the entire roll to be developed.

Because of that factor, I would suggest to roll film shooters to think seriously about bulk loaders. That allows for short film rolls as well as full 36 frame rolls. With ten shots on a roll, it is feasible to shoot for a specific effect, through setting and developing, to achieve the visual effect that the photographer wants. Those photographers following this book are likely to develop their own negatives, thus, it is cheap to keep several ten shot rolls on hand for just that purpose.

Looking through old photographs, especially those shot during the early decades of the twentieth century, shows that most photographers followed the old dictum of negative densities beginning just above the toe. The blacks were deeply rich, yet shadow detail was not prominent. Such a print will look in tonality a bit different than one printed from negatives nestled near the shoulder of the curve. The important aspect of this example is that the photographer has the ability to make that choice at any time by altering the process to fit the need or desire.

Technology has changed, again, advancing photography to yet another frontier; digital imagery. Most photographers today have direct experience using digital photography or digital imagery in some form. It would stand to reason if those photographers have made it this far into this book, they also continue to be interested in traditional photography, using film and chemical developing out procedures. Regardless of how far technology takes digital imagery, using digital recording devices, then digital editing platforms to manipulate and output an image, black and white film photography will live on. It began that march to acceptance during the Secessionist Movement, and through the photogravures seen in Camera Notes.

For those photographers who feel passionate about working within the historical photographic process of using film and projection enlargement to Silver Gelatin prints, I would urge you to take the time to understand the principles of photography. The very tools of your craft. I personally believe that every photographer I have known that have aspired to producing fine art prints, had realized an ideal for themselves, derived from being inspired by one of the masters. A inspirational mentor. Not someone to copy, but someone's work to be emulated.

I have close photographer friends who found Edward Weston as their roll model for what is possible. Others, Ansel Adams, or Paul Strand. For me it was Alfred Stieglitz, including his Camera Notes as well as the fuller Secessionist Movement. That movement, and Alfred's work had to do with a process.

The process of that movement begins with a mindset, that the photography itself is meant as art, and, that the photographer can demonstrate their artistic vision by accomplishing a body of work of archival prints. The, let's see what you got challenge. There are times when digression for the sake of education is more worthwhile than irritating to the reader. I digress here.

The argument all along that photography is not a true art form basically had to do with its mechanical nature, and that 'anyone' can click the shutter and wallah! you have a picture. All that is true of course. Just point the lens somewhere and click. Now it is easy to see that applied to the modern digital camera.

The historical irritation for Alfred arrived with Eastman Kodak's new-fangled roll film camera that could be used to snap photos, then sent back to manufacture to have the photographs printed before being returned for you. It wasn't the cameras nor the technology that garnered the irritation, it was the bike riding camera clubs that went on outings taking snaps, then having them printed, to be hung on gallery walls as art. In that scenario you didn't have to do a thing but click. That irked Alfred.

I have grandkids that have a very good artistic eye, using their digital cameras. They successfully digitally edit their images and print them on an Epson printer, using archival ink. They frame the images and hang them on the wall. Is that Art? It is certainly archival.

In today's world, process works immediately, not in days. Visit any wedding reception or ballroom gathering and notice the several single use digital cameras as part of the party décor. Guests snap shots during the event, then the cameras are taken to a store where they are downloaded into the system and printed while you stand there.

All that is technological advancement. In my thinking, that has nothing to do with fine art photography, nor has it ever. In today's world of high-tech digital servicing, an Edward Weston print, or Eisenstadt print brings a five or seven-digit price tag. Those prints remain art regardless of the technological advances surrounding the photographic method.

I am likely preaching to the choir here, yet feel that too many photographers today do not understand the underlying controls of their craft. Whatever the reason, understanding the characteristic elements of photography is the very thing that leads the photographer to the ability to produce a fine art print, faithfully executed as visualized just before the shutter was clicked.

All the foregoing material as procedure, leads to the final step of the black and white photo process of making the print. How that final print looks depends on the chosen steps in the shooting and developing processes. I will deal with the print as another part of the process. There are entire books dedicated to the print. It is not the scope of this book to attempt such a feat.

The print process does allow for some further, more subtle advancement of the image. Things like print color, tonal range and what I call print signature. Fine Art Printers are much like musicians in that they may play the same instrument, but they put their own spin on the notes played. Their signature. Varying the developing agent alters the resultant print, just like what would be expected when developing negatives. Chemical mixtures have a signature left on the image they interact with.

The primary differences being the chemistry is usually a bit more diluted compared to negatives, and the print paper emulsion is thicker and more absorbent than negatives.

We begin with simple one bath cool toned developers.

Ansco 130:

H_2O @ 115 °F	750 ml	
Metol	2.2 grams	½ + ¼ tsp
Sodium Sulfite (Anhydrous)	50 grams	2 Tbl + ½ tsp
Hydroquinone	11 grams	1 Tbl + ½ + 1/3 tsp
Sodium Carbonate (Anhydrouso	67 grams	3 Tbl + ½ + 1/8 tsp
Glycin	11 grams	1 ½ Tbl + ½ tsp
Potassium Bromide (10% solution)	50 ml	
cold water to make	1000 ml	

~ Use at 70 °F undiluted for maximum contrast
~ Can also be used 1:1 or 1:2 for contrasty negatives
~ For cooler tones replace the bromide with 50 ml Benzotriazole
~ Develop 3-5 minutes

GAF 103: {A favorite}

H_2O @ 115 °F	750 ml		
Metol	3.5 grams	1 tsp	
Sodium Sulfite (Anhydrous)	45 grams	2 Tbl	
Hydroquinone	11.5 grams	1 Tbl + 1 tsp	
Sodium Carbonate (Anhydrous)	67 grams	3 Tbl + ½ + 1/8 tsp	
Potassium Bromide {10% sol)	10 ml	1.2 grams	¼ tsp
cold water to make	1000 ml		

~ Use at 70 °F undiluted for maximum contrast
~ Can also be used 1:1 or 1:2 for contrasty negatives
~ For cooler tones replace the bromide with 50 ml Benzotriazole
~ Develop 3 minutes
~ Very good for contact sheets

GAF 135: Warm Toned Developer

H2o @ 115°F	750 ml	
Metol	1.6 grams	½ tsp
Sodium Sulfite Anhydrous	24 grams	1 Tbl + 1/8 tsp
Hydroquinone	6.6 grams	2 ¼ tsp
Sodium Carbonate (Monohydrate)	24 grams	1 Tbl + 1 tsp
Potassium Bromide	2.8 grams	½ tsp
cold water to make	1000 ml	

*The Potassium Bromide is best kept in 10% solution then used when needed. To equal the gram equivalent = 10 ml of 10% solution per gram weight. For the above formula that would be 28 ml (cc).

~ Use straight for the warmest tonal effect and richest blacks.
~ Dilution 1:1 or 1:2 for more neutral tones
~ Develop 1 ½ to 3 minutes.

GAF 120: Soft Developer

H2o @ 115°F	750 ml	
Metol	12.3 grams	1 Tbl + ½ tsp
Sodium Sulfite Anhydrous	36 grams	1 ½ Tbl + ¼ tsp
Sodium Carbonate Monohydrate	36 grams	2 Tbl
Potassium Bromide [10% sol]	18 ml - 1.8 grams	¼ tsp
cold water to make	1000ml	

Use 1:1 for 1 ½ to 3 minutes
~ Without Hydroquinone this will be a bit cooler toned
~ Increasing Bromide will warm it a bit, towards neutral

The Hydroquinone warms the print tones. Used alone it can offer a warm toned print that emulates the Chloride portrait paper print. One such formula follows.

B-15: Warm tone Single Developer

H20 @ 115 °F 750 ml
Sodium Sulfite (Anhydrous) 85 grams 3 ½ Tbl + ½ + ¼ tsp
Sodium Carbonate (Anhydrous) 113.6 grams 6 Tbl + 1 tsp
Glycin 28.5 grams 7 Tbl
Hydroquinone 9 grams 1 Tbl
Potassium Bromide [10% sol] 40 ml - 4 grams ½ + 1/8 tsp
cold water to make 1000ml

Use 1:7 for rich browns
Use 1:15 for neutral Art Gravure tones
No need to overexpose the paper

Mixing;
1:7 ~ 4 ounces (120 ml) : 28 ounces (840 ml)
1:15 ~ 2 ounces (60 ml) : 30 ounces (900 ml)

B-10: Warm Tone Single Developer

H20 @ 115 °F 750 ml
Hydroquinone 22.5 grams 2 ½ Tbl
Sodium Sulfite 57 grams 2 ½ Tbl + 1/8 tsp
Sodium Carbonate (Anhydrous) 60 grams 3 Tbl + 1 tsp
Potassium Bromide [10% sol] 28 ml - 2.75 grams -½ tsp

Use 1:5
Develop 5-7 minutes at 70 °
Give three times normal exposure on paper before developing

This developer increases the Hydroquinone and decreases the Carbonate accelerator. This increase in quinone will have a warming affect on the print. This formula is used in a less diluted form than the B-15 formula. These two formulas can be used for warming a bromide print.

GAF 113: Amidol Developer

H20 @ 115°F	750ml	
Sodium Sulfite Anhydrous	44 grams	2 Tbl
Amidol	6.6 grams	1 Tbl
Potassium Bromide	.5 grams	1/8 tsp
cold water to make	1000ml	

Use straight then throw away
Develop 1 ½ to 3 minutes at 70°

For those that want to try their hand at printing with Amidol. Amidol is known for creating rich blacks in a bromide print. A primary characteristic of this developer is that it is highly staining. If you get this on your hands it will leave you with black fingertips and fingernails. Use gloves or tongs to manipulate prints in the developer.

Edward Weston's preference for Amidol is a rather good example of a photographer's choice of developers for printing. Amidol is not the only developer that can offer rich blacks, although there are going to be subtle differences in tonal *color,* from warm toned blacks to cooler (blue) toned blacks.

Choosing a print developer is a personal choice, and certainly demonstrates how black and white photographic processing can be used flexibly in shaping the outcome of the final print. Altering the chemistry during negative development as well as print development, directly alters the tonal range of the negative, tonal relationships via densities, sharpness & acutance, tonal range matching between negative & print, and print color

The important thing, is simply remembering that there is no one *best* way in black and white photography. There are numerous ways for expressing a personal photographic vision. The procedures for shooting, with the further application of photo chemistry upon the negative and print, results in a final print which expresses what the photographer wanted to capture in the pre-visualized image. That's the entire point of this book.

Pyrocatechin Developers:

ABC PYRO; Bromide Papers

Solution A:

H2o @ 115°F	750 ml	
Sodium Bisulfite (Anhydrous)	45 grams	½ + ¼ tsp
Sodium Sulfite (Anhydrous)	22.5 grams	1 Tbl
Pyrocatechin	28 grams	1 ½ Tbl + 1 tsp
cold water to make	1000 ml	

Solution B:

H2o @ 115°F	750 ml	
Sodium Carbonate	35 grams	1 ½ Tbl + 1 tsp
cold water to make	1000 ml	

Solution C:

H2o @ 115°F	750 ml	
Potassium Bromide	9.5 grams	95 ml of 10% sol
cold water to make	1000 ml	

Use; 1:2 at 70°
Take 120cc Sol: A & Sol: B added to 240cc water; add 30cc Sol:C
Develop; 1 ½ to 2 ½ minutes

This is a pyro formula that is made for bromide printing papers, which today are the standard. True Chloride papers have gone the way of time. This pyro formula should render good rich blacks in a semi-neutral way. That is, this is not a formula for warming the print tones.

Pyrocatechin ~ Single Bath: Bromide Papers

H_2O @ 115°F	750 ml	
Sodium Bisulfite	2 grams	¼ + 1/8 tsp
Sodium Sulfite	45 grams	2 Tbl
Pyrocatechin	6.25 grams	1 ½ tsp
Sodium Carbonate	45 grams	1 ½ Tbl
Potassium Bromide [10% sol]	60ml- 6.25 grams -1 tsp	
cold water to make	1000 ml	

Use straight at 70°F - 75°F to develop bromide paper
Develop 4-6 minutes; sometimes longer for best results

Two Bath Formulas: Split Bath

Beer's Formula;

Solution A:

H_2O @ 115°F	750 ml	
Metol	8 grams	2 ¼ tsp
Sodium Sulfite	23 grams	1 Tbl
Sodium Carbonate (Monohydrate)	23 grams	1 Tbl + ¾ tsp
Potassium Bromide	1.5 grams	15ml 10% sol
cold water to make	1000 ml	

Solution B:

H_2O @ 115°F	750 ml	
Hydroquinone	8 grams	1 Tbl
Sodium Sulfite	23 grams	1 Tbl
Sodium Carbonate (Monohydrate)	32 grams	1 Tbl + 2 tsp
Potassium Bromide	2 grams	20ml 10% sol
cold water to make	1000 ml	

Use; Contrast Mixing for this formula ~

Low Contrast	Normal Contrast	High Contrast
A: 500 ml	A: 300 ml	A: 125 ml
H20 500 ml	B: 200 ml	B: 875 ml
	H20 500 ml	

2-Bath:

Begin with Metol: 1:32 + 3ml (10% sol) potassium bromide 1 min
Move print to quinone: 1:4 for 2-3 minutes, then final time in Metol bath to desired texture. I do not use this part of the formula.

Freemesser 2-Bath Formula:

Solution A:

H20 @ 115 °F	750 ml	
Sodium Sulfite Anhydrous	58.9 grams	2 ½ Tbl + ¼ tsp
Hydroquinone	24 grams	2 Tbl + 2 tsp
Potassium Carbonate	81 grams	3 Tbl + 1 ¼ tsp
cold water to make	1000 ml	

Solution B:

H20 @ 115 °F	750 ml	
Metol	2.2 grams	½ + 1/8 tsp
Sodium Sulfite	15.2 grams	½ Tbl + ½ tsp
Potassium Carbonate	15.5 grams	½ Tbl + ½ tsp
Potassium Bromide Optional	25 ml 10% solution	
cold water to make	1000 ml	

Use Na2 Co3 (sodium carbonate) for neutral to warmer tones
Use K Co3 (potassium carbonate) for colder tones

The standard instructions call for beginning development in the Metol bath, then move it to the quinone bath, then back to the Metol bath to finish, as shown above. I replicate those instructions here as they came with the formula, however I will also show the method I used, which served me well. The standard instructions are listed under the Beer's formula as I received them. Following is the method I used when printing:

My personal method:

Solution A: Hydroquinone: 1:4 30 seconds to 1 minute; [when strong black appears on zone 2 pull print and rinse 15 secs, then place it in solution B: Metol 1:32 + 3ml ~ 10% solution potassium bromide; leave print until full detail seen in upper tonal ranges: 2-3 minutes.

As can be seen in these two formulas the relationship between the Metol and Hydroquinone solutions alters the outcome of the final print. Increased quinone warms the print, as well as tends to build contrast. Hydroquinone in larger amounts increases the developing energy, hence contrast, as well as warming qualities.

Metol, on the other hand, is a cooler toned developer, much slower in working action and works best for bringing out details in the highlight densities. When moving the print from one tray to the next, the paper is bringing one developer into another as it is already saturated with developer when moved from one tray to the next. This of course begins creating the super-additivity effect.

I have found that the hydroquinone bath works well to develop the blacks almost instantly, in less than thirty seconds. I wait until I see the zone 2 black become evident, then pull the print, wash it for fifteen seconds in the rinse tray, then insert it into the Metol bath until all the detail has developed in the image, which can take 2 to 3 minutes. I also prefer cooling the Metol bath to just below 68°, and warm the hydroquinone bath to just above 70° for best results.

It is this ability to adjust the developing procedure to realize the best print results for each photographer. There is no single correct way to work with black and white photo chemistry. The process possibilities include numerous variations on any formula or procedural practice. This is the beauty of black and white photography. You, the photographer, have the ability to adjust your procedure to arrive at your own signature in printing.

For ease of reference, all the formulas in this book are listed in the last section, under Equivalents ~ Weights & Measures.

Equivalents:
Weights & Measures

Equivalents: Weights & Measures

Equivalents ~ Measures	
1 CC	16.230 minims
5 CC's	81.150 minims
10 CC's	162.30 minims
50 CC's	811.50 minims
100 CC's	1623.0 minims
1000 CC's	1 liter ~ 34 fluid ounces ~ 2 1/8 pint

Weight	DWT Units	1 dwt =1.55 gms = 24 grains
1 gram	15.43 grains	0.6416 DWT
5 grams	77.16 grains	3.21 DWT
10 grams	154.3 grains	6.42 DWT = .32 Troy Ounce
15 grams	231.46 grains	9.644 DWT = .48 Troy
20 grams	308.62 grains	12.859 DWT = .64 Troy
50 grams	771.5 grains	32.14 DWT = 1T:12D:5gr
100 grams	1543.24 grains	6430 DWT = 3T:4D:8gr

Equivalents ~ Weights & Measures

U.S. Liquid Equivalents		Conversion	
1 Gallon	128 fluid ounces	4 Quarts	0.264 Gal = 1.056 quart
		1024 fluid drams	33.8 fluid ounces
		3785.3 CC's	270.52 fluid drams
		3.785 liters	1000 CC's
			1 liter
			1 ml = 22 drops

Avoirdupois to Metric	Metric to Avoirdupois
1 grain = 0.0648 grams	1 gram = 15.4324 grains
2 grains = 0.1296 grams	2 grams = 30.8647 grains
3 grains = 0.1944 grams	3 grams = 46.2971 grains
4 grains = 0.2592 grams	4 grams = 61.7294 grains
5 grains = 0.3240 grams	5 grams = 77.1618 grains
6 grains = 0.38889 grams	6 grams = 92.5941 grains
7 grains = 0.4536 grams	7 grams = 108.0265 grains
8 grains = 0.5184 grams	8 grams = 122.4589 grains
9 grains = 0.5832 grams	9 grams = 138.8912 grains
10 grains = 0.648	10 grams = 154.324 grains

The equivalent measure between ounces, gram weight and grains can be very helpful for converting from chemical weights to formulas using small weight size or older versions of weight measurements. Temperature conversions can also be very helpful for converting temperatures for known developing to different thermometers and their values.

Avoirdupois	Metric Weight
1 pound = 16 ounces	2.2 pounds = 35.22 ounces
7000 grains	15,430 grains
453.56 grams	1000 grams
0.4536 Kilograms	1 Kilo

Temperature Conversions	
Celsius ~ Centigrade ~ {C}	Reaumur ® - Fahrenheit (F)
{C} + (F) 9/5 – T deg C x 332 = T deg (F)	{R}+ (F) 9/4 – T deg R x 32 deg = T deg (F)
(F) + {C} 5/9 {T deg (F) -32 deg} = T deg {C}	{R} + {C} 5/4 T deg {R} = T deg {C}

Materials Mixing procedure	Percent 5%	Solutions 10%
Water (H_2O)	75 milliliters	75 milliliters
Dry Chemical	5 grams	10 grams
Water to Make	100 millimeters (total)	100 milliliters (total)
For a Liter measure (x 10) ~ Of 10% solution 10mls = 1 gram		
10% Solutions - 28% Solution 3 parts Chemical to 8 parts H_2O = 28% solution 1 gram = 10 ml of 10% chemical solution		

Liquid Measure Metric to US	Equivalents US to Metric
1 CC = 16.230 minims	1 ounce = 29.574 CC's
2 CC's = 32.460 minims	2 ounces = 59.147 CC's
3 CC's = 48.690 minims	3 ounces = 88.721 CC's
4 CC's = 64.920 minims	4 ounces = 118.295 CC's
5 CC's = 81.150 minims	5 ounces = 147.869 CC's
6 CC's = 97.380 minims	6 ounces = 177.422 CC's
7 CC's = 113.610 minims	7 ounces = 207.016 CC's
8 CC's = 129.840 minims	8 ounces = 236.590 CC's
9 CC's = 146.070 minims	9 ounces = 266.163 CC's
* 1 US gallon = 3785.43 Cubic Centimeters * 1 Liter = 33 fluid ounces = 394 minims	

Chemical Weight Equivalents in Grams	**1 Tbsp grams**	**½ Tbsp grams**	**1 tsp grams**	**½ t grams**	**¼ t grams**	**1/8 t grams**
Amidol	7	3.5	2.3	1.2	0.7	0.4
Benzotriazole	6	3	2.1	1	0.5	0.25
Borax	15	7.5	5	2.5	1.8	0.7
Boric Acid	12	6	4.1	2	1	0.05
Chlorquinol	9.7	5	3.4	1.7	0.8	0.45
Glycin	4.1	2.1	1.4	0.7	0.35	0.2
Hydroquinone	9	4.5	3	1.5	0.75	0.4
Kodalk	14.5	7.2	4.8	2.4	1.2	0.6
Metol (Elon)	10.5	5.25	3.5	1.75	0.85	0.45
Phenidone	6	3	2	1	0.5	0.25
Potassium Alum	16.8	8.4	5.6	2.8	1.5	0.8
Potassium Bromide	19.5	10	6.5	3.2	1.6	0.8
Potassium Carbonate	24	12	7	3.5	2	1
Potassium Dichromate	22	11.5	7.9	4.1	2.2	1.1
Potassium Ferrocyanide	15.5	8	5.5	2.8	1.5	0.8
Pyrocatechin	16	8	4	2	1	0.5
Silver Nitrate	41	20.7	13.8	7	3.6	1.8
Sodium Bisulfate	22.9	11.5	7.7	4	2	1
Sodium Bisulfite	18	9	6	3	1.5	0.75
Sodium Carbonate	18	9	6	3	1.5	0.75
Sodium Sulfate	22.5	11.4	7.7	3.8	2	1
	1Tbl	½ T	1tsp	½ t	¼ t	1/8 t
Sodium Sulfite	22.8	11.4	7.6	3.8	1.9	1
Sodium Thiosulfate	8	9	6	3	1.5	0.75

13 Parts by weight of Potassium Carbonate ~ equals 10 parts Sodium Carbonate

Table of Solubilities of Photographic Materials			
Substance	Chemical Name	Gram in 100cc of Saturated Sol 40°F	70°F
Alum, Potassium	$K_2\ AL\ (So_4)_4.24H_2o$	6gms	11gms
Alum, Potassium Chrome	$K_2\ Cr_2\ (So_4)_4.24H_2o$	15gms	20gms
Amidol~ Diaminophenol Hydrochloride	$C_6\ H_3\ (OH)(NH_4)\ _2.HCL(1,2,4)$	20gms	25gms
Ammonium Bromide	$NH_4\ Br$	50gms	55gms
Ammonium Carbonate	$(NH_4)_2\ CO_3.H_2O$	25gms	30gms
Ammonium Chloride	$NH_4\ CL$	25gms	25gms
Ammonium Persulfate	$(NH_4)_2\ S_2O_8$	50gms	60gms
Ammonium Thiosulfate (anhy)	$(NH_4)_2\ S_2O_3$	80gms	85gms
Athenon	$C_6H_4(OH)\ (NH.CH_2)\ (OOH)$	Insoluble in H_2o Soluble in alkalis & sodium sulfite	
Borax~ Sodium Borate	$Na_2\ B_4O_7.10H_2O$	2.5gms	7gms
Boric Acid	$H_3\ BO_3$	3.4gms	4.8gms
Metol (Elon)	$C_6H_4(OH)\ (NHCH_3)\ .1/2\ H_2SO_4\ (1,4)$	5gms	8gms
Formalin~ 37% Formaldehyde	CH_2O	All Proportions	
Glycin	Refer to Athenon	Insoluble in H_2o	
Gold Chloride	$AUCL_3.2H_2o$	76gms	>100gms
Hydroquinone	$C_6H_4\ (OH)_2\ (1,4)$	4.25gms	6.25gms
Kodalk		23gms	33gms
Kodelon	$C_6\ H_4\ (OH)\ (NH_2)\ (COOH)_2\ (1,4)$	1.25gms	2.5gms
Lead Acetate	$Pb\ (CH_3CO_2)_2.3H_2o$	30gms	40gms
Mercuric Chloride	$Hg\ Cl_2$	4gms	6gms

Potassium Bichromate	$K_2 Cr_2 O_7$	6.5gms	14gms
Potassium Bromide	K Br	49gms	54gms
Potassium Carbonate (anhydrous)	$K_2 CO_3$	80gms	82gms
Potassium Chloride	K CL	25gms	30gms
Potassium Citrate	$(CH_2COOK)_2.C.(OH) COOK.H_2O$	90gms	100gms
Potassium Cyanide	K CN	44gms	50gms
Potassium Ferricyanide	$K_3 FE (CN)_6$	29gms	35gms
Potassium Hydroxide (Caustic Potash)	*** Can be volatile** K OH	75gms	80gms
Potassium Iodide	K I	95gms	100gms
Potassium Meta-bisulphite	$K_2 So_5$	45gms	55gms
Potassium Oxalate	$(COOK)_2. H_2O$	28gms	35gms
Potassium Permanganate	$K Mn O_4$	3.25gms	6.5gms
Pyrogallol ˜ (Pyro) Pyrogallolic Acid	*** Staining developer** $C_6H_3 (OH)_3$ (1,2,3)	35gms	55gms
Rochelle Salts (Sodium/Potassium Tartrate)	$Na K C_4 H_4O_6. 4H_2O$	49gms	71gms
Silver Nitrate	$Ag NO_3$	105gms	130gms
Sodium Acetate (Anhydrous)	$CH_3 COONa$	30gms	35gms
Sodium Acetate Tri-hydrate Crystal	$CH_3 COONa. 3H_2O$	50gms	60gms
Sodium Bicarbonate	$Na HCO_3$	7gms	9gms
Sodium Bisulfite	$Na HSO_3$ ($Na_2S_2O_5$)	50gms	50gms
Sodium Bromide	Na Br	64gms	70gms
Sodium Carbonate (Anhydrous)	$Na_2 CO_3$	10gms	23gms
Sodium Carbonate (Mono-anhydride)	$Na_2 CO_3.H_2O$	12gms	28gms

Sodium Carbonate (Crystal)	Na2 CO3.10H20	28gms	63gms
Sodium Chloride	Na Cl	30gms	30gms
Sodium Cyanide	Na CN	24gms	46gms
Sodium Hydroxide (Caustic Acid)	*Most caustic chemical Na OH	*boils water when added 48gms	80gms
Sodium Phosphate (Dibasic Crystal)	Na2 HPO4.12H20	6.2gms	23gms
Sodium Phosphate (Tribasic Crystal)	Na3 PO4.12H20	10gms	20gms
Sodium Sulphate (Anhydrous)	Na2 SO4	5gms	20gms
Sodium Sulphate (Crystal)	Na2 SO4.10H20	10gms	40gms
Sodium Sulphide (Fused)	Na S	13gms	17gms
Sodium Sulphide (Crystal)	Na2 S.9H20	35gms	45gms
Sodium Sulfite (Anhydrous)	Na2 SO3	17gms	27gms
Sodium Thiosulfate (Hypo Crystals)	Na2 S2 O3.5H20	70gms	90gms

Equivalent Quantities of Crystalline & Anhydrous Salts	
100 parts by weight of Na2 CO3 .10H20	= 37 ½ parts by weight (Anhydrous Salt)
100 parts by weight of Na2 CO3 .10H20	= 87 ½ parts by weight (Mono-Hydrated)
100 parts by weight of Na2 CO3	= 270 parts by weight (Crystal Salt)
100 parts by weight of Na2 CO3	= 120 parts by weight (Mono-Hydrated)
100 parts Sodium Hydroxide =	133 parts Potassium Hydroxide

100 parts Sodium Hydroxide =	167 parts Potassium Carbonate
100 parts Sodium Hydroxide =	176 parts Sodium Carbonate
3 parts Potassium Alum	2 parts Aluminum Sulphate
Sodium Bisulphite =	Potassium Meta-bisulphite
Sodium Bromide =	Potassium Bromide
Citric Acid =	Tartaric Acid
3 parts Potassium Alum =	2 parts Aluminum Sulphate

Equivalent Quantities of Alkalies	
To neutralize 100 parts by weight of $[K_2SO_5]$ = Potassium Meta-bisulphite	Take of:
Sodium Carbonate (Anhydrous)	Na_2CO_3 ~ 95 parts
Sodium Carbonate (Crystal)	$Na_2CO_3.10H_2O$ ~ 258 parts
Potassium Carbonate (Anhydrous)	K_2CO_3 ~ 124 parts
Sodium Hydroxide	$NaOH$ ~ 36 parts
Potassium Hydroxide	KOH ~ 50 ½ parts

Negative Formulas

Beutler 105

H20 @115° 750 ml (cc)
Metol 5 grams ½ Tbl
Sodium sulfite (Anhydrous) 25 grams 1 Tbl + ¼ +1/8 Tsp
Sodium Carbonate (Anhydrous) 25 grams 1 Tbl +1 1/8 Tsp Cold water to make 1000 ml Qt.

~ Standard dilution; 1:10
~ Developing time; Pan-X ISO 50 - 7 minutes
FP-4 ISO 125 - 8 minutes standard
Tri-X ISO 320/400 = 10 minutes possibly

~ Tank; roll film: continuous agitation for first minute, 15-secs agitation each minute thereafter.
~ Tray; sheet film: continuous agitation throughout development.

[Expansion by concentration & time]
~ Dilution 1:7 (expansion N+1) FP-4 ~ 8 minutes
~ Dilution 1:5 (expansion N+2) FP-4 ~ 8 minutes
~ Dilution 1:10 (expansion N+1) FP-4 ~ 9 minutes
~ Dilution 1:10 (expansion N+2) FP-4 ~ 10 minutes

Fine Grain Developer: D-23

H20 @ 115° 750 ml (cc)
Metol 7.5 grams 2 1/8 Tsp
Sodium Sulfite (Anhydrous) 100 grams 4 Tbl + 1 Tsp
Cold Water to make 1000 ml (cc)

Use; Undiluted {I used it at 1:2}

~ Developing time;	Pan-X ISO 50 - 6 ½ minutes
	FP-4 ISO 125 - 8 minutes standard
	Tri-X ISO 320/400 – 9-10 minutes

~ Tank; roll film: continuous agitation for first minute, 15-secs agitation each minute thereafter.
~ Tray; sheet film: continuous agitation throughout development

Windish Pyro;

Part A:

H2o @ 115°F	750 ml (cc)
Sodium Sulfite	80.0 grams
Pyrocatechin	12.5 grams
Cold Water to make	1000 ml

Part B:

Sodium Hydroxide	(10% solution)

Dilution;	25 ml solution A
	15 ml solution B
	960 ml H2o

FP-4	ISO 125	~ 10 minutes standard
Tri-X	ISO 320/400	~ 13 minutes possibly

~ Tank; roll film: continuous agitation for first minute, 15-secs agitation each minute thereafter.
~ Tray; sheet film: continuous agitation throughout development

Windish; Single Use;

Solution:

To 1 oz H2o	@ 110° Add	3 ml (10% solution) sodium sulfite
	then stir in	¼ Tsp Pyrocatechin
	[Optional]	1/8 Tsp Metol (for super-additivity)
Tank Development;		[24oz] 15 ml solution

Add	735 ml H2o
Add	4.5 ml (10% sol) sodium hydroxide
[16oz]	10 ml solution
Add	490 ml H2o
Add	3 ml (10% sol) sodium hydroxide

Same procedure as above for processing.

Pyrocatechin ~ 2 - Solution (with Sodium Carbonate)
Solution A:

H2o @ 115°	350 ml	
Sodium Sulfite (Anhydrous)	20 grams	½ Tbl + 1 1/8 Tsp
Pyrocatechin	10 grams	2 ½ Tsp
cold water to make	500 ml	

Solution B:

Potassium Carbonate	60 grams	3 Tbl + 1 Tsp
cold water to make	500 ml	

Dilution: Equal Parts A: B
Developing Time; 7 minutes

Pyrocatechin - Tanning:

H2o @ 115°F	750 ml
Sodium Sulfite (Anhydrous)	5 grams
Pyrocatechin	2 grams
Sodium Hydroxide	10 ml (10 % sol)
cold water to make	1000 ml

dilution: Use undiluted

FP-4 ISO 125 ~ 15 minutes standard

Tri-X	ISO 320/400	~ 20 minutes possibly

~ Tank; roll film: continuous agitation for first minute, 15-secs agitation each minute thereafter.
~ Tray; sheet film: continuous agitation throughout development

Pyrocatechin ~ Non-Staining

H2o @ 115°	300 ml
sodium Sulfite (Anhydrous)	50 grams
Pyrocatechin	20 grams
sodium hydroxide	16 grams
Potassium Bromide (restrainer)	2 grams
cold water to make	400 ml

Dilution: 1:10 - 1:15

FP-4	ISO 125	~ 5 minutes standard
Tri-X	ISO 320/400	~ 8-10 minutes possibly

~ Tank; roll film: continuous agitation for first minute, 15-secs agitation each minute thereafter.
~ Tray; sheet film: continuous agitation throughout development

D-76:

H2o @ 115°F	750 ml
Metol	2 grams
Sodium Sulfite Anhydrous	100 grams
Hydroquinone	5 grams
Kodalk	2 grams
cold water to make	1000 ml

Dilution:

General use 1:1

Film Type A ~ 25-50 ISO	7 minutes
Film Type B ~ 100-125 ISO	9 minutes
Film Type C ~ 320-400 ISO	11 minutes

This formula is the only MQ developer listed in this book. It is to give the reader insight into the differences between these two types of developing agents. This formula is likely the most popular commercial developer to ever be used. I make no guarantees however.

Notice in the formula the 2 grams of Metol, and the 100 grams of sodium sulfite, which is very close to the D-23 formula. The 5 grams less of Metol is replaced with the same amount of hydroquinone, with Kodalk to buffer the extra oxidation taking place from the superadditivity of the combined reducing agents. This formula then becomes a higher energy developer than the Beutler formula. Hence the compensating effect of Butler's softer working development.

Stop Bath & Hardening Formulas

Chemicals	SB1 AN216	SB3	170	172 D25
Acetic Glacial Acid	17 grams			6.5 ml 10% sol
Potassium Alum (Chrome Alum)		30 grams		15 grams
Potassium Metabisulphite			50 grams	
Water To Make	1000 cc	1000 cc	1000 cc	1000 cc

Hypo Remover: Negatives

Sodium Carbonate or Bicarbonate 10% solution
Use 5 minutes then wash ten minutes

Hypo Remover: Paper Prints

Water (Distilled)		20 ounces	500 cc
Hydrogen Peroxide	3% solution	5 ounces	125 cc
Ammonia	3% solution	4 ounces	100 cc
Water to make		40 ounces	1000 cc

Hypo Remover: Dilution

H_2O @ 125°F	750 ml
Sodium Sulfite	200 grams
Sodium Bisulfite	2 grams
C	

Dilute: 1:9 for use
Use 5 minutes then wash ten minutes

Fixing Baths

Non-Hardening fixing Baths:

#158 Rapid Fix

H_2O @ 125°F	750 ml
Ammonium Thiosulfate (Crystals)	150 grams
Sodium (or) Potassium Metabisulfite	20 grams
cold water to make	1000 ml

Clearing Time:

Negatives ~ 1 1/2-2 minutes ~ Full fixing time; 4 minutes
Prints ~ 1 minute ~ Full fixing time; 5 minutes

#159 Acid Fix

H_2O @ 125°F	750 ml
Sodium Thiosulfate (Crystals)	250 grams
Sodium Sulfite (Anhydrous)	10 grams
Acetic Acid	15 grams
cold water to make	1000 ml

Clearing Time:

Negatives ~ 2-3 minutes ~ Full fixing time; 6 minutes
Prints ~ 4-5 minutes ~ Full fixing time; 10 minutes

Acid Hardening Fixing Baths:

F15/PIF;

H_2O @ 125°F	750 ml
Sodium Thiosulfate (Crystals)	240 grams
Sodium Sulfite Anhydrous	15 grams
Acetic Glacial Acid (28% solution)	48 ml
Boric Acid	7.5 grams
Potassium Alum (hardener)	15 grams
cold water to make	1000 ml

Clearing Time:

Negatives ~	2-3 minutes ~	Full fixing time; 6 minutes
Prints ~	4-5 minutes ~	Full fixing time; 10 minutes

F6;

H_2O @ 125°F		750 ml
Sodium thiosulfate	(Crystals)	240 grams
Sodium Sulfite	(Anhydrous)	15 grams
Acetic Glacial Acid	(28% solution)	48 ml
Kodalk		15 grams
Potassium (Chrome) Alum		15 grams
cold water to make		1000 ml

Clearing Time:

Negatives ~	2-3 minutes ~	Full fixing time; 6 minutes
Prints ~	4-5 minutes ~	Full fixing time; 10 minutes

ATF5 ~ Rapid Acid Hardening Bath

H2o @ 125°F	750 ml
Ammonium Thiosulfate (Crystals)	200 grams
Sodium Sulfite (Anhydrous)	15 grams
Acetic Glacial Acid (28% solution)	55 ml
Boric Acid	7.5 grams
Potassium (Chrome) Alum	15 grams
cold water to make	1000 ml

ATF2 ~ Rapid Acid Hardening Bath

H2o @ 125°F	750 ml
Ammonium Thiosulfate (Crystals)	112 grams
Sodium Sulfite (Anhydrous)	15 grams
Potassium (Chrome) Alum	15 grams
cold water to make	1000 ml

Clearing Times in Sodium Thiosulfate

C. I. Jacobson ~ "Developing" [C. E. K. Mees]

Sodium Thiosulfate %	13°C 55°F	18°C 65°F	24°C 75°F
	Time in Minutes		
10.00%	(Longer Than) 10	9 ½	7
15.00%	8	7 ½	5
20.00%	6	4 ½	4

Clearing Times in Sodium and Ammonium Thiosulfate

C. I. Jacobson ~ "Developing" [C. E. K. Mees]

Concentration	{at 20 °C) Sodium Thiosulfate Time in Minutes	Ammonium Thiosulfate Time in Minutes
10%	7	2
20%	5	1 ½
30%	3 ½	½
40%	3 ½	½

When to Change Fixing Bath

C. I. Jacobson ~ "Developing" [C. E. K. Mees]

Size of Film	Number Per Liter
8x10 Sheet Film	25
4x5 Sheet Film	100
6cm x 9cm Sheet Film	150
120 Roll Film	25
35mm Roll Film (36 Exposures)	25

Print Formulas

Ansco 130:

H20 @ 115 °F		750 ml	
Metol		2.2 grams	½ + ¼ tsp
Sodium Sulfite Anhydrous		50 grams	2 Tbl + ½ tsp
Hydroquinone		11 grams	1 Tbl + ½ + 1/3 tsp
Sodium Carbonate Anhydrous		67 grams	3 Tbl + ½ + 1/8 tsp
Glycin		11 grams	1 ½ Tbl + ½ tsp
Potassium Bromide	10% solution	50 ml	
cold water to make		1000 ml	

~ Use at 70 °F undiluted for maximum contrast
~ Can also be used 1:1 or 1:2 for contrasty negatives
~ For cooler tones replace the bromide with 50 ml Benzotriazole
~ Develop 3-5 minutes

GAF 103: {A favorite}

H20 @ 115 °F	750 ml	
Metol	3.5 grams	1 tsp
Sodium Sulfite Anhydrous	45 grams	2 Tbl
Hydroquinone	11.5 grams	1 Tbl + 1 tsp
Sodium Carbonate Anhydrous	67 grams	3 Tbl + ½ + 1/8 tsp
Potassium Bromide {10% sol)	10ml	1.2 grams-¼ tsp
cold water to make	1000 ml	

~ Use at 70 °F undiluted for maximum contrast
~ Can also be used 1:1 or 1:2 for contrasty negatives
~ For cooler tones replace the bromide with 50 ml Benzotriazole
~ Develop 3 minutes
~ Very good for contact sheets

GAF 135: Warm Toned Developer

H2o @ 115°F	750 ml	
Metol	1.6 grams	½ tsp
Sodium Sulfite (Anhydrous)	24 grams	1 Tbl + 1/8 tsp
Hydroquinone	6.6 grams	2 ¼ tsp
Sodium Carbonate (Monohydrate)	24 grams	1 Tbl + 1 tsp
Potassium Bromide	2.8 grams	½ tsp
cold water to make	1000 ml	

*The Potassium Bromide is best kept in 10% solution then used when needed. To equal the gram equivalent = 10 ml of 10% solution per gram weight. For the above formula that would be 28 ml (cc).

~ Use straight for the warmest tonal effect and richest blacks.
~ Dilution 1:1 or 1:2 for more neutral tones
~ Develop 1 ½ to 3 minutes.

GAF 120: Soft Developer

H2o @ 115°F	750 ml	
Metol	12.3 grams	1 Tbl + ½ tsp
Sodium Sulfite (Anhydrous)	36 grams	1 ½ Tbl + ¼ tsp
Sodium Carbonate (Monohydrate)	36 grams	2 Tbl
Potassium Bromide [18 ml of 10% sol]	31.8 grams	¼ tsp
cold water to make	1000ml	

Use 1:1 for 1 ½ to 3 minutes
~ Without Hydroquinone this will be a bit cooler toned
~ Increasing Bromide will warm it a bit, towards neutral

The Hydroquinone warms the print tones. Used alone it can offer a warm toned print that emulates the Chloride portrait paper print. One such formula follows.

B-15: Warm tone Single Developer

H2o @ 115 °F	750 ml	
Sodium Sulfite (Anhydrous)	85 grams	3½ Tbl+½+¼ tsp
Sodium Carbonate (Anhydrous)	113.6 grams	6 Tbl + 1 tsp
Glycin	28.5 grams	7 Tbl
Hydroquinone	9 grams	1 Tbl
Potassium Bromide [10% sol]	40ml - 4 grams	½ + 1/8 tsp
cold water to make	1000ml	

Use 1:7 for rich browns
Use 1:15 for neutral Art Gravure tones
No need to overexpose the paper

Mixing;
1:7 ~ 4 ounces (120 ml): 28 ounces (840 ml)
1:15 ~ 2 ounces (60 ml): 30 ounces (900 ml)

B-10: Warm Tone Single Developer

H2o @ 115 °F	750 ml	
Hydroquinone	22.5 grams	2 ½ Tbl
Sodium Sulfite	57 grams	2 ½ Tbl + 1/8 tsp
Sodium Carbonate (Anhydrous)	60 grams	3 Tbl + 1 tsp
Potassium Bromide [10% sol]	28 ml	2.75 grams ½ tsp
cold water to make	1000ml	

Use 1:5
Develop 5-7 minutes at 70 °F
Give three times normal exposure on paper before developing

This developer increases the Hydroquinone and decreases the Carbonate accelerator. This increase in quinone will have a warming effect on the print. This formula is used in a less diluted form than the B-15 formula. These two formulas can be used for warming a bromide print.

GAF 113: Amidol Developer

H_2O @ 115°F	750 ml	
Sodium Sulfite Anhydrous	44 grams	2 Tbl
Amidol	6.6 grams	1 Tbl
Potassium Bromide	.5 grams	1/8 tsp
cold water to make	1000ml	

Use straight then throw away
Develop 1 ½ to 3 minutes at 70°F

For those that want to try their hand at printing with Amidol. Amidol is known for creating rich blacks in a bromide print. A primary characteristic of this developer is that it is highly staining. If you get this on your hands it will leave you with black fingertips and fingernails. Use gloves or tongs to manipulate prints in the developer.

Pyrocatechin Developers:
ABC PYRO; Bromide Papers

Solution A:

H_2O @ 115°F	750 ml	
Sodium Bisulfite (Anhydrous)	45 grams	½ + ¼ tsp
Sodium Sulfite (Anhydrous)	22.5 grams	1 Tbl
Pyrocatechin	28 grams	1 ½ Tbl + 1 tsp
cold water to make	1000 ml	

Solution B:

H_2O @ 115°F	750 ml	
Sodium Carbonate	35 grams	1 ½ Tbl + 1 tsp
cold water to make	1000 ml	

continued next page

Solution C:

H_2O @ 115°F	750 ml
Potassium Bromide	9.5 grams 95 ml of 10% sol
cold water to make	1000 ml

Use; 1:2 at 70°F
Take 120cc Sol: A & Sol: B added to 240cc water; add 30cc Sol:C
Develop; 1 ½ to 2 ½ minutes

Pyrocatechin ~ Single Bath: Bromide Papers

H_2O @ 115°F	750 ml	
Sodium Bisulfite	2 grams	¼ + 1/8 tsp
Sodium Sulfite	45 grams	2 Tbl
Pyrocatechin	6.25 grams	1 ½ tsp
Sodium Carbonate	45 grams	1 ½ Tbl
Potassium Bromide [10% sol]	60ml-6.25 grams	1 tsp
cold water to make	1000 ml	

Use straight at 70°F - 75°F to develop bromide paper
Develop 4-6 minutes; sometimes longer for best results

Two Bath Formulas: Split Bath
Beer's Formula;

Solution A:

H_2O @ 115°F	750 ml	
Metol	8 grams	2 ¼ tsp
Sodium Sulfite	23 grams	1 Tbl
Sodium Carbonate (Monohydrate)	23 grams	1 Tbl + ¾ tsp
Potassium Bromide	1.5 grams	15ml 10% sol
cold water to make	1000 ml	

continued next page

Solution B:

H20 @ 115°F	750 ml	
Hydroquinone	8 grams	1 Tbl
Sodium Sulfite	23 grams	1 Tbl
Sodium Carbonate (Monohydrate)	32 grams	1 Tbl + 2 tsp
Potassium Bromide	2 grams	20ml 10% sol
cold water to make	1000 ml	

Use; Contrast Mixing

Low Contrast	Normal Contrast	High Contrast
A: 500 ml	A: 300 ml	A: 125 ml
H20 500 ml	B: 200 ml	B: 875 ml
	H20 500 ml	

2-Bath:

Begin with Metol: 1:32 + 3ml (10% sol) potassium bromide 1 min
Move print to quinone: 1:4 for 2-3 minutes, then final time in Metol bath to desired texture. I do not use this part of the formula.

Freemesser 2-Bath Formula:

Solution A:

H20 @ 115°F	750 ml	
Sodium Sulfite (Anhydrous)	58.9 grams	2 ½ Tbl + ¼ tsp
Hydroquinone	24 grams	2 Tbl + 2 tsp
Potassium Carbonate	81 grams	3 Tbl + 1 ¼ tsp
cold water to make	1000 ml	

continued next page

Solution B:

H20 @ 115 °F	750 ml	
Metol	2.2 grams	½ + 1/8 tsp
Sodium Sulfite	15.2 grams	½ Tbl + ½ tsp
Potassium Carbonate	15.5 grams	½ Tbl + ½ tsp
Potassium Bromide *Optional	25 ml 10% solution	
cold water to make	1000 ml	

Use Na2 Co3 (sodium carbonate) for neutral to warmer tones
Use K Co3 (potassium carbonate) for colder tones

The standard instructions call for beginning development in the Metol bath, then move it to the quinone back, then back to the Metol bath to finish. The standard instructions are listed under the Beer's & Fremeiser formulas in Part 4: The Print.

Below is the method I used when printing:

Split bath developer: Sol A first then Sol B;

Solution A: Hydroquinone: 30 seconds to 1 minute; when black shows strong on zone 2, remove the print and place it in wash tray for 15 seconds, then place it in Solution B: Metol: leave print until full detail seen in upper tonal ranges: 2-3 minutes.

*Add 3ml - 10% solution potassium bromide [for any fogging];

Dilution to Dilution Chart:

~ Diluting a % solution to another % is not difficult. This is used when it is desirable to dilute a 27% solution to a 20% solution.

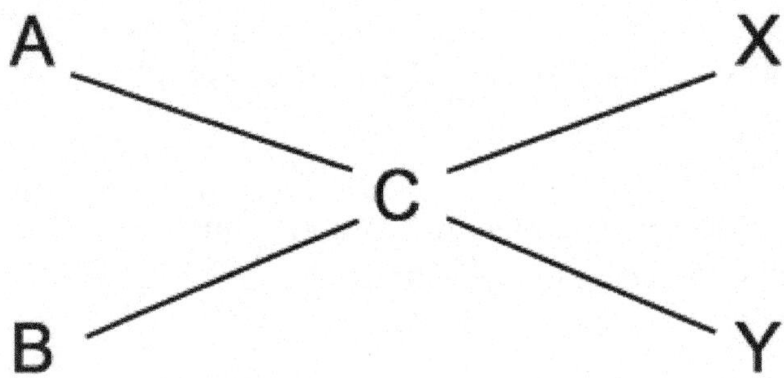

A = the % dilution of the solution to be diluted.
B = the % dilution of the diluting solution
(* If water is used for this value the value is 0)
C = the % dilution desired
X = C - B
Y = C - A

Solution:

~ Place at A the % strength of the solution to be diluted
~ Subtract C from A and place at Y
~ Subtract B from C and place at X
* If B is water the value is '0'
~ Take X parts of A ~ Y parts of B and mix to equal C

Cut Film Holder Covers; For Texture Tests

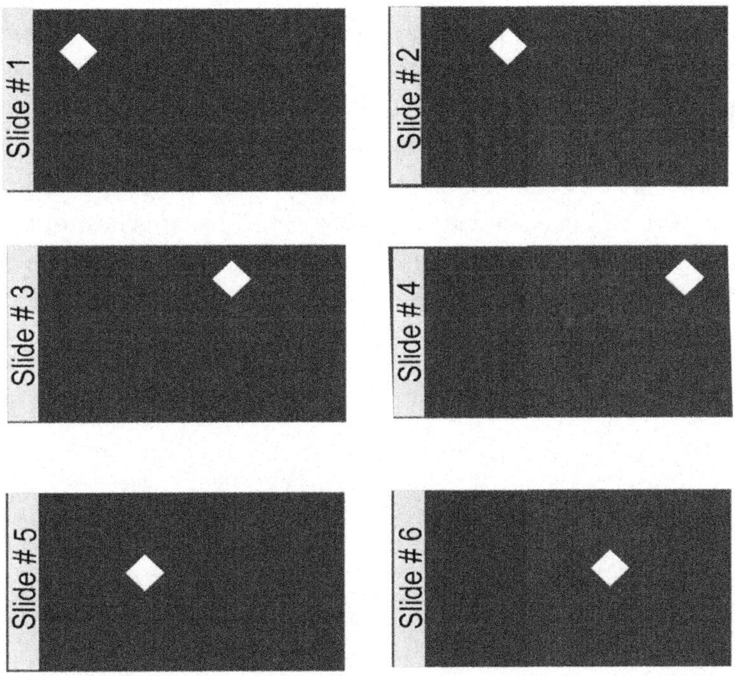

The above diagram shows one means of shooting texture tests for a format camera. I chose a very thin plastic type material that could be cut with scissors. I cut out six dark slides for my 5x7 cut film holders. Each was cut so the "Slide # strip" showed when the dark slide was inserted. The first four become the final four by flipping the covers over to place the new diamond spot at the bottom row. Place tape on the flip side continuing the number system to ten.

There are two methods for exposure holes. The first is simply making ten slides with one diamond cut per slide, or any shape you fancy really. Use an exacto knife to cut out the shapes. I used six slides, with the first four each having four diamond cuts on the first row, then two more slides with diamond cuts in the middle row, offset to the first row. After those six shots, I merely flipped the first four slides over to place the final four diamond cuts onto the film along the bottom row, mirroring the first row.

This gives you ten distinct density patterns to look at for one texture text on a film to be developed. Best practice for roll film is bulk film loaders to allow for ten shot rolls for such tests. The process is the same for roll film, by simply using each frame as one shot, advancing each image with a commensurate change with the shutter/aperture to increase each shot by one shutter speed reduction, [more light] or opening one stop of the aperture. You will need at least eight test shots, but it is best to take ten, which allows you more information on the upper densities which are the densities most affected by developing time.

Bibliographic References

Bibliographic References

D-76, *Photo-Lab Index*, Supplement No. 172, p.24

D-76, *The Film Developing Cookbook*, Stephen G. Anchell And Bill Troop, p. 40-44.

D-76H (Formula #19), *The Darkroom Cookbook, 2nd Edition*, Stephen G. Anchell, p. 154.

"Developing" Focal Press London & New York 1940-1966;
C. I. Jacobson, PhD. The negative technique.

"The Keepers of Light", William Crawford, Morgan & Morgan, Dobbs Ferry, New York; 1979.

"Encyclopedia of Photography", Edited by Bernard E. Jones, Arno Press, New York; 1974.

Brother Coyote Publications
ISBN - 13: 978-0692453476
ISBN -10: 0692453474
B.C.P

Printed in Great Britain
by Amazon

61534094R00087